Penrith is an ideal centre from which to experience the pleasures of walking, and the surrounding countryside provides a variety of scenery which can be enjoyed in peace, away from the crowds of the Lake District.

The scenery constantly changes throughout the year, from the rich verdant greens of Spring and throughout summer to the golden glory of Autumn. And from heather clad fells to snow-capped Pennine hills on frosty winter mornings. All this can be experienced and enjoyed by following the walks in this book, published by the Penrith Group of the Ramblers Association.

The author has personally walked each of the routes described, which have been recommended by different local walkers. The meticulous attention to detail should mean that even inexperienced walkers can set out on any of the routes described with confidence, in the knowledge that by following the instructions carefully, they will enjoy a wonderful experience.

The Penrith Group of the Ramblers Association is a very active group with a programme of walks throughout the year. These include day walks every Wednesday and Saturday, graded easy to strenuous, and during the summer months the group provides shorter walks on Thursday evenings.

For further information please contact **www.penrithramblers.org.uk** or see the current programme of walks in the local library. Should you feel inspired to join the Group you will receive a very warm welcome and as a member of the Ramblers Association you will be able to walk with groups throughout the country.

Charles Hirst

Charles Hirst
Chairman

Contents

Ullswater & the Eamont Valley

The Lowther Valley

The Eden Valley 3

North and West of Penrith 4

Leith & Lyvennet Valleys 5

Using the maps

All the maps in this guide are from the OS Explorer series 1:25,000 scale and, with the odd exception, are used full size for maximum clarity.

The routes are defined by a coloured line overlay which is translucent so that you can see the public rights of way classifications on the map. Where the route departs from a recognised path a white dotted line has been added to show the way. This dotted line has also been added to routes in and out of Penrith to help navigate through the streets.

The numbered orientation points on the maps correspond to route descriptions in the text. We recommend that you stop at each numbered point and familiarise yourself with the route ahead both on the map and from the text before moving on.

Walk gradings used in this book

Easy walks will generally be on clear paths or grassland with ascents and descents at a measured and leisurely pace

Moderate graded walks will be of a good length and may include some fairly steep climbs and rougher moorland

Strenuous walks will be more challenging and include steep climbs and rough country

Walking tips

Choose footwear in which you'll be comfortable walking over uneven and possibly wet terrain. Walking boots are especially fine as they also provide ankle support.

Weather here can change quickly and dramatically. Take a weather check before you go and don't rely entirely on a sunny outlook. It might be wise to pack an extra layer or so to keep you warm and dry if conditions change.

You may well find that there are places to buy refreshments on route, but do add a few energy giving snacks and a full water bottle to your rucksack.

Take your mobile phone which can be useful in an emergency, Reception can be patchy or non-existent here and there.

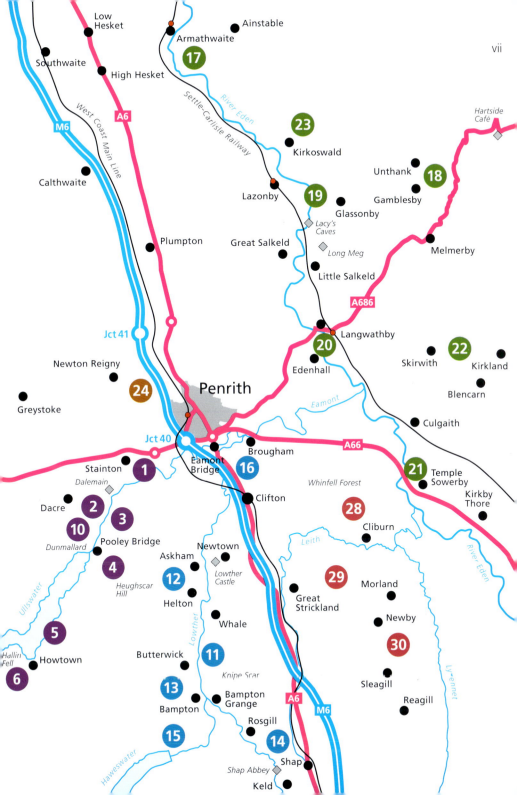

Walking
around **Ullswater**
and the
Eamont Valley

ramblers
at the heart of walking

Town, field and Eamont riverside paths plus a visit to Mayburgh Henge

FACTFILE

Distance
8 miles (12km)
Cumulative height: 250 ft
Our rating: Easy

Getting there
Regular public transport to
Penrith from Carlisle, Kendal,
Keswick and several towns and
villages in Eden. Car parking in
and near the town centre.

Local services
Several cafés, restaurants and
public houses in Penrith;
tearoom, public house and
restaurant in Stainton; public
houses in Eamont Bridge.

Start grid NY515301

Map
OS Explorer OL5, English Lakes
north-eastern area

The walk commences from Penrith Market Square. The Market Square lies in the centre of the town and contains the 1861 Musgrave Monument Clock Tower. The walk passes out of the town via Castle Park and traverses various field paths to Stainton village. It then drops down to the River Eamont and uses riverside paths to Eamont Bridge, with a diversion to explore Mayburgh Henge. It returns to Penrith town centre via pedestrian routes through Pategill and along Bishops Yard by St Andrews Church.

The Walk

1 Locate Angel Lane which leads in a westerly direction off the Market Square between Bakewell's and Northern Goldsmith's shops. Proceed along the Lane, then from the other end cross over the car park/market area of Great Dockray. At the far side locate Gordon Clark's butchers shop and the adjoining covered entranceway to Fallowfield Court. Continue up the shallow steps through the court. At the exit from the court cross diagonally right over the junction with West Lane and continue uphill along Neville Avenue to reach a small green at the top of the rise. Turn right here along Castle Terrace to reach steps and a gate at the entrance to Castle Park.

2 Once in the park continue a few yards to a path junction *[Note: from this junction you may wish to cross the bridge and explore Penrith Castle.]* Turn sharp left and meander through the park. At the further side make towards the 'Black Angel' memorial to those who died in the Boer War. From the memorial cross over the bandstand green to reach an exit gateway from the park, then continue between dwellings to reach Castle Drive.

The construction of **Penrith Castle** began in 1399, when William Strickland, later to become Bishop of Carlisle and Archbishop of Canterbury, added a stone wall to an earlier pele tower, primarily as a defence against Scottish raids. The Neville family added the Red Tower early in the 15th century and from 1471 Richard, Duke of Gloucester, transformed the castle by adding a new gatehouse and an impressive range of lodgings around the courtyard, before he became King Richard III in 1483. The ruins that can be seen today date from about that time.

The castle remained part of the Crown Estate until the reign of William III who gave it and most other Crown property in Cumberland to his friend Hans Willem Bentinck, 1st Earl of Portland. The castle eventually passed from the Earls and Dukes of Portland to the Dukes of Devonshire who sold it to the Lancaster & Carlisle Railway Company who built Penrith railway station. It later passed into the ownership of the Penrith Urban District Council who in the 1920s converted the grounds into a public park and built housing nearby. The castle is maintained now by English Heritage.

The Black Angel in Castle Park

3 Turn right, cross over the road and after a short distance turn off left between houses onto a path signed: *Public Footpath Skirsgill Gardens*. Proceed along this path with the wall to Queen Elizabeth Grammar School on the right side. By a bend turn right, off the path and climb over a wall stile into the grammar school grounds, again signed to *Skirsgill Gardens*. Cross over the playing fields, keeping tennis courts at first on the left then across a playing pitch. At the far side climb over another stile onto the A592 road, Ullswater Road. Cross straight over the road via the traffic island then turn left and walk along the pavement. Turning gradually right, pass by the entrance to Cranstons Food Hall, the garage forecourt and then Atkinsons DIY store and continue along the grass lined pavement of Haweswater Road. Pass under the West Coast main line then turn off right and back onto a rising public footpath, signed to *Stainton*.

Scale: 4cm = 1km (0.6 mile)

4 Go up steps then cross over the M6 motorway on the bridge alongside the railway. Once across veer right up some steps, then right again, along an enclosed path. Pass by one field then turn left, off the path and climb over a stile into a field. Proceed along the left side of the field and after passing through a former field divide turn diagonally right to the opposite side of the field. Once across, turn left and continue down the right side of the field and over a stile in the lower corner, onto Mile Lane.

5 Cross Mile Lane and climb over a stile onto the continuation of the footpath, signed to *Stainton*. From the stile veer diagonally right to a stile in the right field wall. Once over this stile veer diagonally left to the further side of the field then turn left and follow the right field boundary to a gate and stile in the further corner. Continue ahead along the right side of the next field to a wall stile about half way along its length. Climb over the stile and again proceed diagonally left across the next field to its further edge and turn left. Follow the right boundary to a gate at the further corner. Pass through the gate and turn right along an enclosed green lane. Pass under a bridge of the former Penrith to Keswick railway after which the lane becomes a metalled access road. Just in advance of reaching the A66 road turn off to the right along an enclosed track that leads to a gate. Pass through the gate and continue along a rough track that winds a little as it crosses some pastures, with the former railway route to the right side. Pass by various separate agricultural buildings and through gates, keeping the railway route on the right side. Upon reaching a farm yard turn left, keeping on the track and shortly reach a gate that leads onto the back country road from Stainton to Penrith.

6 Turn left and continue along this road, then pass under the A66 road into Stainton. Pass by some houses and a farm shop/tearoom to shortly reach the main village cross roads. Cross the junction onto the village street, signed towards *Ullswater*. Pass by the village hall then the Brantwood Hotel on the left. After a further few yards turn off left onto an unsigned 'no through road' (The first property on the right in this road is called 'Mains Cottage'). After passing some dwellings turn off left onto a signed *public footpath*. Climb over two stiles and continue along the right side of a narrow paddock before climbing over a further (gated) stile. From this stile veer right, across a pasture, to a stile set at the foot of a wooded bank. Climb over this stile, rise up the bank and climb over a further (gated) stile at the top of the bank. From here veer left, across the corner of a field to a further stile. Climb over this stile, cross a small planted area then over a stile to reach the Stainton road once again and turn right.

7 Walk along the road for about 200 yards then turn off right along an enclosed track. Follow this track gently downhill, cross over the A592 road then continue downhill more steeply, now signed as a *Byroad*. At the foot of the hill the track reaches the River Eamont. At this point turn left and climb over a stile onto a footpath signed to *Yanwath* and *Tirril*.

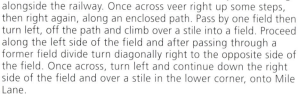

Views to Cross Fell

Stainton

Continue along this path, close to the river and after two further stiles enter a wooded area beneath a limestone scar. Once in the wood rise up a number of hillside steps, then descend again towards the river and follow through to a further stile at the woodland edge. Continue then along riverside pasture to reach a gated footbridge across the river.

8 **Cross the footbridge** and turn left along a path signed to Yanwath. Keep on the river side of a fence then pass through a gate and onto a wooded path, again signed to *Yanwath*, that runs close to the river along the lower slopes of a bank. After passing through the wooded area reach a stile and footbridge across Lady Beck, then pass through a gate into a field. Continue along the left edge of the field to a further footbridge and gate (or stile) at the foot of a steep bank. Once through the gate rise up the bank and over a stile into a higher level field. Continue along the left edge of the field, over another stile and along the left edge of the next field to a further stile. From this stile again keep along the left edge of the next field, but at the further corner climb over the stile on the left (or through the gate) then continue in the same direction as before, but with the field boundary now on the right side. At this point a good view of the C14th & C15th Yanwath Pele Tower and Hall can be gained. Once at the further side veer left to a stile (and gate) that leads onto the Yanwath Hall access road close to the bridge under the West Coast Main Line.

✱ Diversion route anticipated until at least 2011

[Note: the footbridge crossing the River Eamont, described at point 8, is closed, awaiting repairs, following flood damage. Until this work is completed the following temporary diversion can be used. This route can also be used as a short-cut option.]

8✱ **Turn left at the footbridge** and proceed uphill through a series of five fields. The route then passes through a foot tunnel beneath the West Coast Main Line. Continue along an enclosed path and through a gate that leads onto the verge of the A66 Trunk Road.

9✱ **Turn right along the verge** to Junction 40 Interchange roundabout. Use pedestrian lights to cross the A66 and the Motorway slip roads, then proceed along the left side of the A592 road towards Penrith town centre. At the first roundabout the outward route will be reached. Cross to the pavement in front of the filling station and retrace your route back to Penrith Market Square and the end of the walk.

River Eamont

Yanwath Hall comprises a well preserved C14th pele tower and a C15th hall, reputed to be the finest manorial hall in England. It has changed little since the 16th Century. In 1671 the property passed to the Lowther family and from that time onwards has been used as a farm. The Hall was the birthplace of William Wordsworth's Quaker friend Thomas Wilkinson, poet and writer (1751-1836). It is to him that Wordsworth addressed 'To the Spade of a Friend'. The battlemented tower measures 39 feet by 30.5 feet in size and has walls 5 feet thick.

Eamont Bridge

9 Turn right, go under the bridge then turn sharp left into the access leading to the property 'The Grotto'. A direction sign is located on the railway retaining wall. Pass through a gateway then turn right onto an enclosed path. Pass through two gates and onto the right edge of a long field. Continue along the edge of the field, which narrows then widens slightly, to reach a stile (and gate) at the further end. Once over the stile proceed along the left edges of three fields, separated by gates, to reach a gate in the left edge of the third, close to the boundary of the M6 motorway. Turn and pass through the gate then drop gently down, beside the motorway, to reach the access to Southwaite Green Mill residential country park. Turn right, pass under the motorway then right again, along the access road. Pass by a footpath on the left, signed to *Eamont Bridge* and continue along the access road past two groups of residential properties. After passing the last property, named Ash Lea, continue to the entrance gate on the left that leads into the Ancient Monument of Mayburgh Henge.

10 Explore Mayburgh Henge then turn right, from the entrance gate and retrace your steps along the access road back to the footpath, signed to *Eamont Bridge*. Turn right and climb over the stile onto an enclosed path that runs at first alongside a residential property. Pass through a gate, then with a hedge at first to the left and fence to the right continue for about 400 yards to reach a further gate that opens onto the metalled access road to the property Bleach Green. Turn right, along the access road and after about 300 yards reach the A6 road beside the ancient Eamont Bridge.

11 Cross straight over the A6, beside the traffic lights. Pass through a metal gate, then cross the River Eamont by the pedestrian bridge. Once over, continue ahead and uphill on the pavement to the A6. At the Kemplay roundabout between the A6 and A66 veer around to the right. Don't cross any carriageways but leave the roundabout along a short metalled footpath that leads to the cul-de-sac end and turning area of a road associated with Carleton Hall police headquarters.

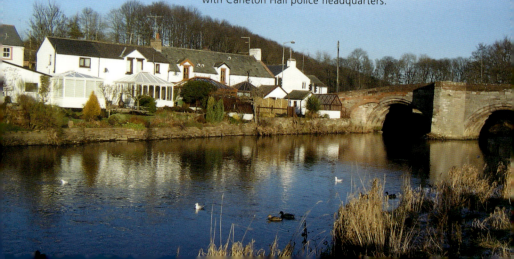

Continue gently downhill along the pavement of this road with a carriageway of the A66 to the left side. Turn left, under the A66, to reach a junction with the A686 Penrith to Alston road. Cross this road and turn right along the left pavement for a distance of about 200 yards.

12 Just short of a road junction on the left turn off left, behind houses, onto a path signed *Public Footpath Pategill*. This path opens into a vehicular rear property access. Cross the access area and at the next road turn right, then left into the cul-de-sac Carleton Hall Walk. Continue to the head of the cul-de-sac then turn left and up steps between dwellings. At the head of the steps pass between dwellings then cross a road diagonally right into Mary Langley Way. Pass between more dwellings then continue ahead from the road's turning head along a pedestrian route called Hargreaves Court. Cross Pategill Square, veer right then left across Lonsdale Court and complete the pedestrian route by reaching Pategill Road. Turn right, along the road, then left into the first court on the opposite side. Cross over the turning circle of the court then leave by a narrow metalled path that turns right, behind a dwelling to reach the main route of Carleton Road.

Mayburgh Henge is a large Neolithic henge dating from between 2000 and 1000BC and may have been a meeting place for a prehistoric community. It consists of a single circular bank, up to 6.5 metres high and 50 metres across its base, broken by a single entrance and enclosing an area with a diameter of some 90 metres. The bank, estimated to contain 1 million stones, is constructed of pebbles collected from the nearby river. In the centre is a single monolith of volcanic ash 2.8 metres high. Back in the 18th century there were four standing stones in the centre, and a further four at the entrance. These other stones were destroyed in 1720.

Penrith. Looking across the rooftops to St Andrew's Church

13 Cross diagonally right into the narrow 'exiting' section of Folly Lane. Proceed along the right side of the road, which has no pavement at first. Later, keep along the pavement, at times elevated a little above the road. Eventually reach the junction of the road with Friargate and Benson Row. Turn left here, on the outside of the junction to regain the right pavement. Once Friargate car park is reached turn off right, across the right edge of the car park. Continue ahead into the pedestrian route which encircles St Andrews churchyard, here signed as Bishop Yards. Follow this route around to a T junction at the front of the church. Turn left to reach Penrith Market Square and the end of the walk.

Historic routes, parkland and buildings in the vicinity of Ullswater

The walk begins from the small village green in the centre of Dacre village, opposite the driveway to Dacre Castle. Upon leaving the village it follows the old route past the Castle to Dalemain. It then crosses parkland and continues beside the River Eamont to Pooley Bridge. From the shores of Ullswater it ascends into high plantations before following a route across undulating farmland past Bennethead, Sparket Mill and Hutton John. The return to Dacre follows above the valley of Dacre Beck before descending dramatically back to the village.

The Walk

1 Commence the walk by crossing the road from the village green, then pass through a gate onto a track which is signed as a *Public Footpath*. After a short distance cross a cattle grid (gate adjoining) then pass alongside Dacre Castle.

Dacre Castle is a pele tower and was built in the 14th Century with walls seven feet thick and 66 feet high for protection against the Scots. Marauding was dying out in the 17th century and the castle was then made more habitable by the fifth Lord Dacre, who added the large windows. When the Earl died in 1715 his possessions were sold off and the castle was then bought by Edward Hasell. It remains part of the Hasell estate of Dalemain.

Scale: 4cm = 1km (0.6 mile)

Dacre derives its name from 'the trickling one' by reference to Dacre Beck. Dacre church is largely 12th century, with 15th and 19th century additions. The churchyard contains four 'bear' statues, which represent stages in a story, the meaning for which is not known. In the first stage a bear stands alone. In the second an animal approaches the bear from behind. In the third the bear and the creature wrestle. The fourth and final stage shows the bear by itself with a satisfied smile on its face.

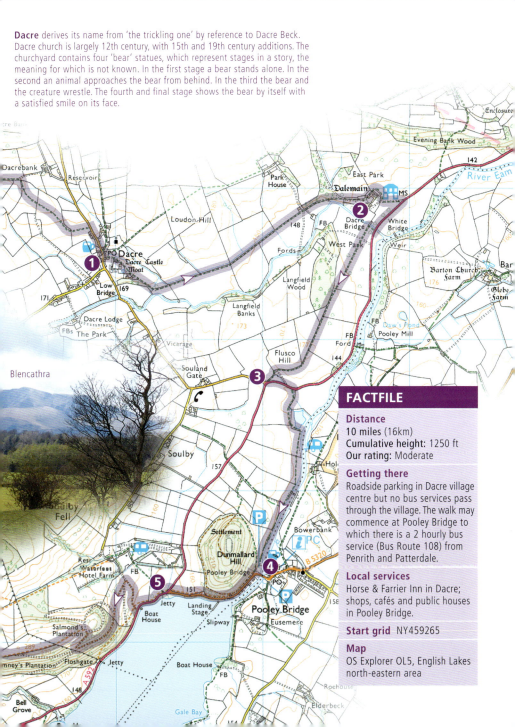

FACTFILE

Distance
10 miles (16km)
Cumulative height: 1250 ft
Our rating: Moderate

Getting there
Roadside parking in Dacre village centre but no bus services pass through the village. The walk may commence at Pooley Bridge to which there is a 2 hourly bus service (Bus Route 108) from Penrith and Patterdale.

Local services
Horse & Farrier Inn in Dacre; shops, cafés and public houses in Pooley Bridge.

Start grid NY459265

Map
OS Explorer OL5, English Lakes north-eastern area

There has been a settlement at **Dalemain** since Saxon times, when a fortified pele tower existed. The cobbled courtyard reflects the defensive nature of the settlement that surrounded the tower. The Old Hall was added in the 14th century, together with another tower. In the 16th century two projecting wings were added, creating a typical Elizabethan manor house. In 1744, the Georgian frontage was constructed to enclose an inner courtyard. Very little change has been made to the buildings since those times.

From the Castle veer slightly to the left with the track then drop downhill and turn around to the left to reach a gate and stile. Continue along a straight section of track for about a quarter of a mile and pass through two gates in close succession. The track then provides a further straight section of about a third of a mile (through a gateway at about the half way point) to reach another combination of two gates in quick succession. From these gates continue up a rise by woodland, then drop down again between garden walls associated with Dalemain, to arrive in a cobbled courtyard to the rear of the house.

2 Turn left and leave the courtyard under a stone archway, along a metalled access driveway. Cross a cattle grid (gate adjoining) then continue along the driveway, curving round to the right, past the main car park. Cross another cattle grid (gate adjoining), continue around to the left to reach the main access cattle grid and gate, then turn right at the junction onto the verge of the A592 (Penrith to Patterdale) road. Walk along the verge for just over 250 yards (the front of Dalemain House will be clearly visible from here) then, after crossing the bridge over Dacre Beck, turn off right, over a stile and onto a signed *Public Footpath*. From the stile proceed straight ahead a short distance, as far as the end of the older stone arched Dacre Bridge. Turn left at the bridge, onto a clear grassy path and continue along this path, rising uphill through Dalemain West Park for about three quarters of a mile, to reach a gate and stile near the top of the rise. Continue then to a second gate and stile, just past woodland, then on, with a fence to the right side, to reach a third such combination. From here the path drops downhill, keeping a fence on the right side. At the foot of the hill climb over a stile, then continue ahead to a stile and gate that leads onto a junction with the A592 road.

3 Turn left, along the A592 road, then after about 200 yards turn off right, through a kissing gate onto a footpath signed *Pooley Bridge 3/4 mile*. Drop down to a footbridge, then proceed along the left side of a field. Cross a second footbridge to reach a stile and gate on the left at the field corner. Once over, drop downhill beside a fishing lake to a gate set in the right fence close to the River Eamont. Pass through this gate onto a path which lies close to but parallel with the river. Continue along this path as it traverses the lower riverside edges of four fields, separated by gates. At the further edge of the fourth field pass through a gate into riverside woodland. Keep the River Eamont on the left side and shortly cross the car park to reach the B5320 road beside Pooley Bridge.

[Note: The walk can be started from this point which is served by the 2 hourly 108 bus service to and from Penrith. The bus sets down and picks up in the village centre on the opposite side of Pooley Bridge.]

4 At the car park entrance turn right and pass through the gate into the woodland at the foot of Dunmallard Hill. *[Note: If you are just starting the walk here just keep ahead to the gate from the end of Pooley Bridge].* Once through, turn left along the path signed *Permitted Path: Circular Route, Dunmallard Hill*. Follow this path, which remains close to the woodland edge and the B5320 road. At a path junction bear left on the route signed as a *Permitted Path* to *Waterfoot* and shortly after veer right, at another junction, to avoid dropping down to the road. Pass through a gate at the woodland edge then continue along the inner edge of a roadside thicket with a field to the right side. The path then emerges from the thicket at the road junction between the A592 and B5320 roads. Cross over the A592 ahead, turn left for a short distance, then right, off the road and through a gate onto a path signed *Permitted path: Floshgate 1/4 mile, Bennethead 1 mile*.

Pooley Bridge lies alongside the River Eamont at the northern end of Lake Ullswater. The name Pooley Bridge is derived from the earlier existence of a large pool in the River Eamont, just where it flows out of Ullswater, giving the name Pooley. In the 16th Century, a bridge (above) was built across the river, hence Pooley Bridge. The pool has now disappeared, whilst the bridge remains. Pooley Bridge used to be a small fishing and farming community.

Dunmallard woodland

5 Turn left, once through the gate and proceed along the left edge of a field, parallel with the road. Pass through a gate, then continue along the edge of the next field as far as a grass centred track which commenced at a nearby road gate. Turn sharp right and follow this track uphill for about 200 yards to a point where it approaches a fence corner at a track/path junction. Turn sharp left in front of the fence and continue uphill on a signed grassy path, curving slightly towards the left to reach a stile at the edge of the hillside wood of Salmond's Plantation. Once over, continue along a steadily rising path through the plantation. Climb over a second stile and turn sharp right then, after rising up a little further, turn sharply round to the left at direction signs. Continue uphill to reach a further stile at the upper level of the plantation. From the stile continue along the left edge of a field with woodland immediately to the left side. Climb over a stile, veer away to the right from the woodland to a nearby track and follow this downhill then right, around the outside of a field corner. Keep a fence to the right side to shortly come alongside a barn, then turn left and downhill at the field corner beside the barn. Upon reaching a gate and kissing gate on the right side pass through, then cross diagonally left over a field brow and through a gate beside woodland. Drop down steeply, cross Ramps Beck by stepping stones, then rise up the right edge of the next field and through a further gate onto the Dacre to Bennethead road.

6 Turn left, along the road and into Bennethead hamlet. *Bennethead means: The high place where holly grows.* Pass by the farm and turn right, along a road signed to **Penruddock** and **Greystoke**. Proceed along this road for about a third of a mile then turn off left at a bend, onto a metalled access road (the first you come to). Pass through three gates along this road, then dog leg right, through the hamlet of Tongue. Pass through a further gate and continue uphill along a poorly surfaced track. Upon approaching a further gate and ranch fencing, turn sharply to the right (at right angles), off the track and cross a field to a stile. Once over, continue ahead to a further stile that leads into the wooded area around the property Land Ends. Turn right from the stile, then left at a sign and over a footbridge. Continue ahead through woodland and over a second footbridge. Again continue ahead across more open scrubland, cross a third footbridge and reach a gate that opens into a field, at the far left corner. From the gate continue ahead and gently downhill along the left sides of two fields, separated by a stile, to a stile near the further left corner of the second. Climb over the stile and continue along a short section of right field edge to a further stile. Once over, drop down onto the access road at Grovefoot Farm. Turn sharp right, then left, and pass along the concrete access road, in front of the farmhouse.

7 Pass to the left of a barn to reach a gate just beyond the farm buildings. Pass through and veer slightly left, across the left corner of a field and over a footbridge and stile. Continue ahead, across the right diagonal of the next field to a stile in the further corner and the Dacre to Thackthwaite road at the property 'Sparket'. Turn right, along the road and pass by the property, then turn off left through a gate, onto a signed Public Footpath.

Proceed along the left side of a field and through a gate at the further corner. From here the path is enclosed for a little then continues along the right side of a field and over a stile. It then turns to the right in the next field and crosses to ford a gill and reach a gate. Pass through the gate, then continue ahead to a stile at the further field side that leads onto the Bennethead to Penruddock Road. Turn left, along the road, and shortly reach a road junction beside Sparket Mill.

8 Veer right and keep along the road at Sparket Mill, pass across a second road junction and rise uphill beside the plantation that surrounds Hutton John. Where the trees end (about half a mile from Sparket Mill) turn off right, over a stile, onto a public footpath signed *Dacre 1¹/₃ miles*. Proceed ahead and over a stile set to the left side of a barn. Once over, the footpath continues along the right sides of three fields, separated by stiles and gates. *[Note: From the first field a good view can be gained back towards Hutton John and its grounds.]* From the stile and gate at the end of the third field the route continues ahead along the upper left side of the fourth field, then after a further stile/gate combination continues as a track which dips, then follows along the right side of the fifth. Turn right close to the end of this field (within sight of Dacrebank Farm) and climb over a wall stile into another field. Veer left across the upper level of this field to a stile on the further side. Once over continue ahead and downhill veering slightly to the right to come alongside a further field boundary near the foot of the field. At a corner turn left and through or over a stile/gate combination, then contour ahead across the next field to reach a wall stile at the further side. Climb over the stile onto the A66 to Dacre road and turn right. Continue downhill to reach Dacre village once again and the end of the walk at the village green.

[Note: If you have commenced the walk from Pooley Bridge continue by following the descriptions in paragraphs 1 to 3, to return to your starting point.]

Sparket Mill

Hutton John began life as a pele tower. The major part of the house is Jacobean, constructed in the 1660's. The township of Hutton John was formerly held as part of the Barony of Greystoke and passed to the Huddleston's in the reign of Queen Elizabeth 1. The property became the only residence of the family following confiscations by Oliver Cromwell.

Hutton John and Little Mell Fell

Field paths and fellside overlooking
the River Eamont and Ullswater.

FACTFILE

Distance
5⅓ miles (8.5km)
Cumulative height: 650 ft
Our rating: Moderate

Getting there
Public transport from Penrith or
Glenridding - 2 hourly (Bus route
108) to Barton road end. Car
parking in front of Barton Church,
200 yards from road end.

Local services
Shops, cafés and public houses in
Pooley Bridge; inn at Tirril village,
near Barton.

Start grid NY488263

Map
OS Explorer OL5, English Lakes
north-eastern area

The walk begins by St Michael's church at Barton. It then
rises up paths onto the northern end of the long High Street
range of fells to provide widespread views of the eastern
Lake District and across the Eden Valley towards the North
Pennines. It descends to the picturesque village of Pooley
Bridge and then returns to Barton along field paths close
to the River Eamont.

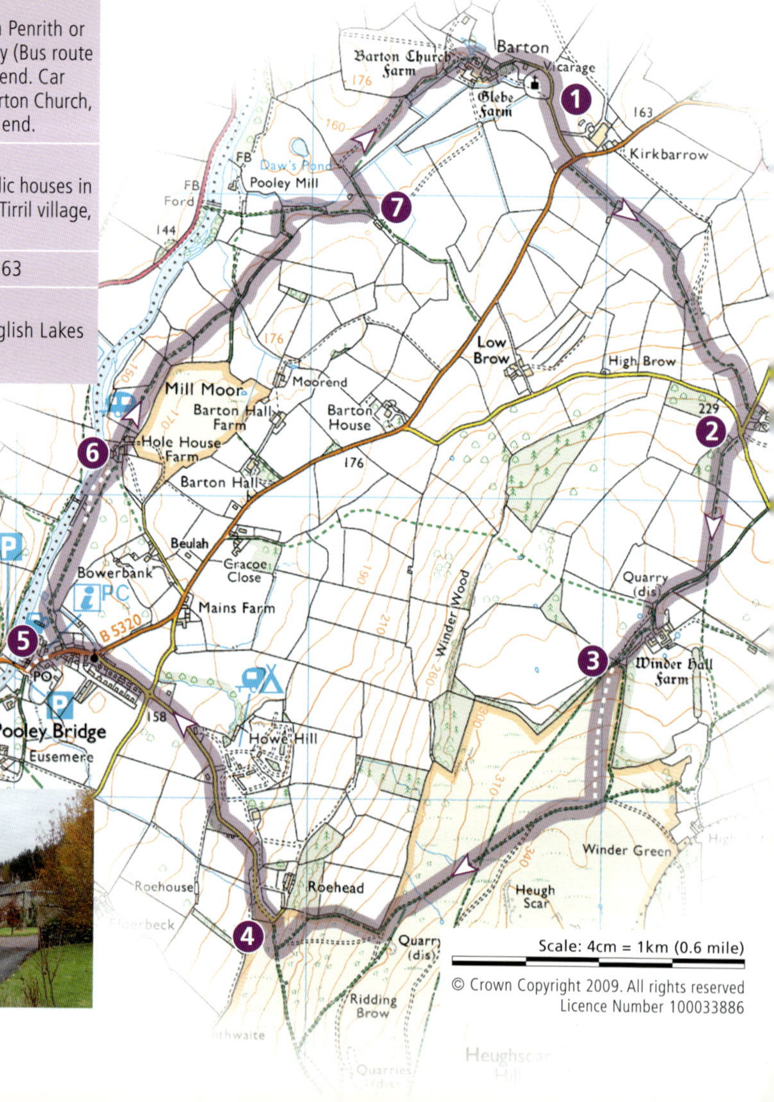

Roehead

Scale: 4cm = 1km (0.6 mile)

The Walk

1 From the Lych gate to Barton Church proceed along the access road to reach the B5320 (Tirril to Pooley Bridge) road after about 200 yards. Turn right, then cross over the road to a stile (and gate) that leads onto a public footpath signed to *Celleron*. Continue along the left side of a field, pass through a gate and then along the left edge of the next field to reach a gate (and stile) at the further upper corner. Once through the gate rise quite steeply uphill ahead, past a former limekiln to the left, to a further stile. Veer left and continue uphill from the stile to round the outside of a field corner. Keep a fence on the right side and at the top edge of the field reach a further stile (and gate) that leads onto the road at Celleron. Turn right, along the road, and after a few yards cross over a road 'T' junction to a gate that leads onto a public footpath signed *High Winder 1/2 mile*.

2 From the gate proceed along the right side of a long field and rise up gently to reach a ladder stile at the further upper corner. From the stile turn right, along the farm access road to Winder Hall Farm (Low Winder). Pass by a residential property to the right then the walled farm complex to the left and reach the gate(s) that leads onto the open access Heughscar fell land.

Winder Hall Farm was previously known as Low Winder. The building, which is identified as an Ancient Monument, dates from 1572. Winder is derived from 'windy shieling', with both High and Low Winder being in windy locations.

Winder Hall Farm

3 From the gate continue ahead along a stony rising path. This path, which might be a little boggy in places, rises up parallel with a shelter belt of trees on the left side. Shortly after the shelter belt is passed a cross junction of paths is reached close to a structure on the hillside that houses a water storage tank. Turn right at this junction onto a grassy track that contours a little below the skyline of the Heughscar hillside. The track passes over a hill brow as it turns around to the left and the limestone crag of Heugh Scar comes into view just over the brow. Once over the brow, and before reaching the Scar veer right, off the track, onto a narrow grassy path that leads gently downhill towards Ullswater and a wall corner at the left end of a prominent line of trees. Continue along this path to the wall corner, turn right and with the wall on the immediate right side drop downhill towards Pooley Bridge. Where a coniferous woodland is reached on the right, turn left and continue along the now grassy track and drop down to reach a wide stony track. Turn right, along the track and after about 100 yards reach a gate that leads onto the head of the metalled road at Roehead.

4 From Roehead continue downhill along the road, past several wayside seats, for about half a mile to reach a junction with the road to Howtown. Cross over this junction and continue past houses, a church and another road junction (with the B5320 road), to reach the centre of Pooley Bridge.

In the vicinity of **Heughscar Hill** widespread views can be gained of the eastern Lake District fells. A diversion to the top of the Scar would also open up views to the east of Penrith, the Eden Valley and the North Pennines.

Approach to Pooley Bridge

The name **Pooley Bridge** is derived from a pool (in the River Eamont) by the hill, to which 'bridge' was added later. The village is popular with tourists, given its location close to Ullswater. Here there are various facilities, including an information centre and cafés.

Pooley Bridge and Dunmallard

Hole House Farm

5 From the centre of the village retrace your steps the short
distance back to 'The Sun' inn. Turn left off the road beside the
inn, to reach a gate that leads onto flat pasture land. Pass through
the gate and continue along a gravel track. This passes through
a second gate and later changes to a grassy surface as it traverses
the pasture land beside the waste water treatment works. It then
continues to a further gate, close to the River Eamont. Pass
through the gate into a planted area, with a riverside seat.
Continue gently uphill and pass through another gate to reach
gates that lead onto the concrete apron of Hole House farm
complex.

6 Traverse the length of the complex and pass through a
gate onto a field track. At the far side of a first field pass through
another gate. Continue along the grassy track across a second
and once a fence line comes up from the left and turns, keep
this then on the immediate left side to reach a further gate in
the field corner. Turn left, through this gate, then after a few
yards turn right, through another gate onto an enclosed green
lane. Turn left, along the lane to reach a further gate at the far
end and once through cross the top right edge of a field to reach
another gate. Pass through this gate and within the next field
veer left, then skirt around to the right below a shallow hill
shoulder, to reach a stile and gate in the upper right corner. Once
over the stile continue along the right edge of the next field to
reach a rough track and wooden path signpost on the further
side.

7 Turn left along the track which is signed as a *Bridleway* to
Barton. Pass through two gates then after a few yards turn right,
again along a track, again signed to *Barton*. Continue along this
track for about a quarter of a mile, passing through a gate, then
over a ladder stile (adjoining gate). A short distance after the stile
the track turns right, into the Barton farm complex. To pass
through the complex turn left, in front of the first building. Next,
turn right between farm buildings and pass through a stone
archway, under which a gate is located. Once through the archway
and gate pass to the left of some dwellings to reach a junction
close to Glebe Farm. Turn left and continue along the metalled
access road from the junction and after passing the old rectory
for Barton church return, once again, to the Lych gate and the
end of the walk.

Barton was never a village, the name
deriving from 'buildings belonging to
a farm'. The Norman Church of St
Michael occupies a site on a mound
with a circular churchyard that may
have prehistoric origins. The Lych gate
was built as a memorial to those lost
in the two world wars. The church
contains several memorials to relatives
of the poet William Wordsworth.

St Michael's Church, Barton

A walk around the limestone escarpment of Heugh Scar with uninterrupted views of the Ullswater environs

The walk begins by the memorial in the centre of Pooley Bridge village, five miles south-west of Penrith on the B5320. From this attractive riverside village, close to Ullswater, the walk provides a steady ascent to the adjoining fell from which widescale views of Penrith, the Lake District, the Eden Valley and North Pennines can be gained. The later descent offers a panorama of the Eamont Valley and landscapes of northern Cumbria. The walk returns through pastures beside the River Eamont itself.

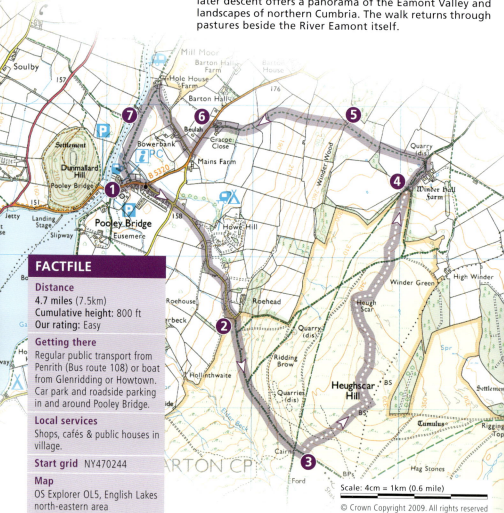

FACTFILE

Distance
4.7 miles (7.5km)
Cumulative height: 800 ft
Our rating: Easy

Getting there
Regular public transport from Penrith (Bus route 108) or boat from Glenridding or Howtown. Car park and roadside parking in and around Pooley Bridge.

Local services
Shops, cafés & public houses in village.

Start grid NY470244

Map
OS Explorer OL5, English Lakes north-eastern area

Scale: 4cm = 1km (0.6 mile)

The Walk

1 From the centre of the village, and with your back to the bridge over the River Eamont, walk along the road towards Penrith passing by the Sun Hotel on your left. At the mini roundabout veer right, with the church and village hall on the right and once past the village dwellings reach a crossroads. Walk straight ahead at the crossroads, signed to *Hillcroft*, pass the entrance to a camping/caravan site on the left and continue up the hill to Roe Head. Here the road ends at a gate leading onto Barton Fell Common.

2 Pass through the gate onto a good, rough surfaced track, signposted *Bridleway* to *Helton*. Continue walking steadily uphill for about half a mile, ignoring cross paths, until you reach a prominent cairn (a pile of stones) on the right of the track at a path junction. From this junction continue ahead for a further 40 or so paces then turn left onto a grassy rising path between bracken. Follow this path steadily uphill to eventually reach the summit area of Heughscar Hill. At this point turn left onto a grassy path amongst some exposed limestone. *[Note: At this point you will notice another grassy path ahead to a cairn, which marks the very top of Heughscar Hill. It is suggested that if you visit the cairn you should then retrace your steps back to this point.]*

Limestone Scarp, Heughscar Hill

Heughscar Hill has an elevation of 1231ft. Its name is interpreted as being 'the rocky scarp on the heel-shaped hill'. The main rocky outcrop on this hill is called Heugh Scar.

Barton Fell and Ullswater

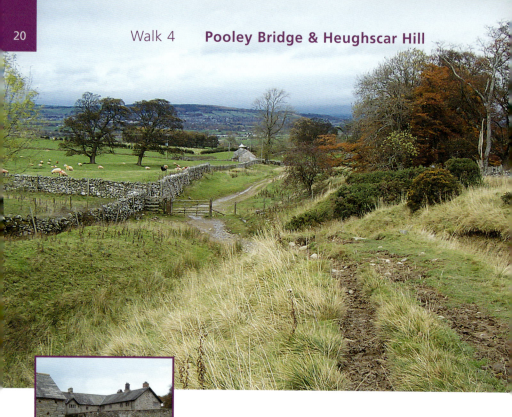

Winder Hall Farm was previously
known as Low Winder. The building,
which is identified as an Ancient
Monument, dates from 1572. Winder
is derived from 'windy shieling', with
both High and Low Winder being in
windy locations. The course of High
Street Roman Road, which ran south-
west for 19 miles from Brougham to
Troutbeck, is thought to pass up the
drive to Winder Hall Farm and then
across the moorland below Heughscar
Hill and onwards to Barton Fell,
Loadpot Hill and High Street. Where
traceable on the ground the route
might be discernible as an agger (low
rampart), terraceway or a simple
hollow way.

3 Proceed along the path, skirting the summit area, above
a small escarpment. Follow the path gently around to the right
keeping close to the escarpment top but being sure not to
descend below the escarpment. The path eventually passes
above the rocky limestone crag of Heugh Scar. Once across this
crag do not descend with the steep path ahead but turn off
right onto a narrow faint path which leads to a junction with
a wider grassy hilltop path. Upon reaching the wider path turn
left then follow this path across the rear section of Heughscar
Hill to reach a junction with a major cross path. Cross over this
junction and continue along a lesser path making gradually
towards a plantation of deciduous trees to the right. At a shallow
path junction veer left and continue gently downhill across
somewhat boggy ground, now parallel with the trees, to reach
a kissing gate at the hill foot, close to Winder Hall Farm.

4 Pass through the gate then continue along a farm track.
Pass by Winder Hall on the right and a cottage on the left. Once
past the cottage turn left, through a gate, into a field. Continue
gently uphill along the right side of the field with a stone wall
then a wire fence boundary. Climb over a stone wall stile at the
upper end of the field then continue ahead gently downhill.
Pass to the right of some odd trees and a small ponded area
and once over the hill brow reach a ladder stile.

5 Descend steeply ahead from the ladder stile to reach a footbridge and stile on the lower side of the next field. Once over this stile cross a further field diagonally to your left to reach a stile near the bottom left corner. Climb over this stile then with a fence to the right side follow along the field edge to reach a gate (and stile) that leads into a short enclosed lane. Follow along the lane and pass by a small group of houses to reach the B5320 road.

6 Turn left and walk down the road for a short distance before turning right into a minor road signposted *Hole House Farm*. Follow the minor road, passing close to the back of some houses on the left. At the end of the garden wall there is a metal kissing gate. Go through the gate then turn right, across the flank of some meadowland keeping fairly close to a caravan site. Once past the site turn to the right towards a gate close to Hole House farmstead. Do not go through the gate but turn sharp left onto another path that leads towards the River Eamont. Pass through a gate, drop downhill through woodland, then through another gate to regain the meadowland close to the river.

7 Continue ahead, parallel with the river, along a grassy, then stony track the length of the meadowland. At the far side pass through a gate into a smaller paddock area then another gate, then continue up the side of the Sun Hotel to reach the main street at Pooley Bridge. Turn right along the street and return to the memorial and the end of the walk.

The old School House at Barton

The path down from Heughscar

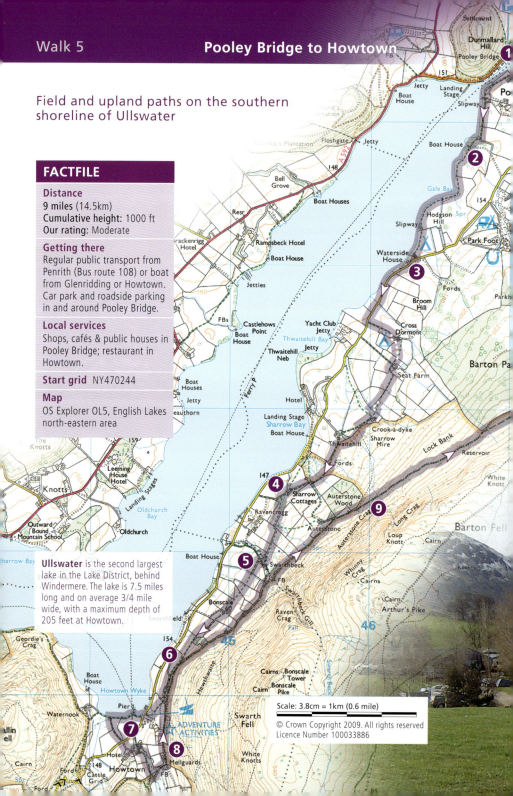

Field and upland paths on the southern
shoreline of Ullswater

FACTFILE

Distance
9 miles (14.5km)
Cumulative height: 1000 ft
Our rating: Moderate

Getting there
Regular public transport from
Penrith (Bus route 108) or boat
from Glenridding or Howtown.
Car park and roadside parking
in and around Pooley Bridge.

Local services
Shops, cafés & public houses in
Pooley Bridge; restaurant in
Howtown.

Start grid NY470244

Map
OS Explorer OL5, English Lakes
north-eastern area

Ullswater is the second largest
lake in the Lake District, behind
Windermere. The lake is 7.5 miles
long and on average 3/4 mile
wide, with a maximum depth of
205 feet at Howtown.

Scale: 3.8cm = 1km (0.6 mile)

The walk begins by the memorial in the centre of Pooley Bridge village, five miles south-west of Penrith, on the B5320.

From this attractive riverside village, close to Ullswater, the walk firstly traverses the lower field paths within view of the lake. It turns at Howtown and returns to Pooley Bridge by a series of higher level paths within Open Access Land amongst the foothills of Barton Fell and Heughscar Hill. Wide panoramic views of Ullswater and beyond can be gained from several parts of the walk.

The walk passes Howtown Pier, close to its halfway point. There are regular boat services to and from Pooley Bridge from the pier. These might be used if only half the walk is to be tackled.

The Walk

1 From the monument in the centre of the village commence the walk towards the bridge, with the village shop on the right side. Where the road turns to cross the bridge keep ahead and pass between sandstone pillars onto the 'Private Drive' for Eusemere Lodge. Walk along the drive then, at a junction, turn right onto a path signed *Public Footpath: Waterside House 1¼ miles*. Pass through a gate and follow a gravel path gently downhill towards the edge of Ullswater. Once close to the shore pass by the front of a large boat shed and around the end of a wall. From the wall rise up a little and continue along a path at the top of a shore-side embankment, parallel with the lake. Where this path reaches a track, bear down right to a gate which is close to the shore beside a rough access launch ramp.

Waterside House

Shoreline path

2 Pass through the gate onto a shoreline path across pasture land. Continue across a footbridge and pass by a former boat house to a gate at the pasture edge. Once through the gate the path crosses some boggy ground by means of a board walk. It then passes round Gale Bay, utilising the shingly surface of the lakeshore and a footbridge, to reach a gate at the edge of a camping and caravanning site. Pass through the gate and continue along a gravel path through the site. The path traverses a low lakeside mound, Hodgson Hill, then passes through another gate close to a boatyard and slipway. From the gate continue across the site, close to the lake and pass to the right side of farm and camping site buildings. Upon reaching Waterside House turn up left, in front of the house signed *Footpath End: Use Road* to reach the Pooley Bridge to Howtown road.

Hodgson Hill is an ancient earthwork, thought to have been a Viking fortified shore settlement. The settlement would have accommodated up to 200 armed Vikings.

3 Turn right, along the road, for just over a quarter of a mile to reach a farm drive on the left signed *Public Footpath: Cross Dormont*. Proceed up the farm drive then, upon almost reaching the first building, turn sharp right (yellow direction sign) to a gate and stile which also contains a Public Footpath sign. Once over, veer left and uphill to a further gate, stile and sign. From here veer right, across the field, towards a caravan site and a stile which is set in the fence. Once over the stile continue along the left field boundary to a gate by the entrance to Seat Farm and the caravan site. Pass through the gate and cross over the farm entrance onto a track signed *Public Footpath: Howtown Road via Crook-a-dyke*. Pass through another gate and turn around left to a stile. Climb over the stile then traverse the left edge of a field. At the far corner pass left, over a stone stile then traverse the right edge of the next field. At the further side the path turns and crosses a ford to reach a gate at Crook-a-dyke. From the gate pass in front of the property, where a slate sign will be noticed directing to Howtown and Martindale. Continue along the drive to a point where a gate is located in the left wall and another sign directs to Howtown and Martindale. Pass through this gate onto open land and immediately turn right. Follow a path through gorse and bracken, keeping a wall to the right side. The path passes by the property Thwaitehill then veers left at a junction with another path that emerges from this property.

Sharrow Cottages

Bonscale Pike

Keep a wall on the right side and when this turns sharply right continue ahead between gorse and bracken. Cross a ford beside a wall that comes in from the left, then climb over a stile into a small enclosed area. At the further end reach a track and gate, then continue ahead along a grass centred track that leads downhill towards Sharrow Cottages.

4 Pass by Sharrow Cottages then veer off the track to the left and uphill along a grassy path amongst trees, to reach a stile. Once over, continue along the upper left side of a field to a further stile. Climb over this stile, turn left and over a further stile. Turn right, along the right lower edge of a field. Pass through a gate and shortly after drop down to a further gate beside woodland with the property, Swarthbeck, ahead. From this gate continue along a short stretch of enclosed track, cross a bridge over Swarthbeck Gill and reach a path junction immediately in front of the property. Turn right and upon rounding the building end cross a drive and grass mound to a stile *[note - this might be partially hidden by equipment]*.

Swarthbeck

5 Climb over the stile and proceed along the left upper edge of a field. Pass through a gateway and continue ahead across a second field to a gate. From the gate cross a ford and a third field to another gate, then ahead across a fourth to reach a further gate, hard up against the property Bonscale. Pass through the gate and cross in front of the property to another gate. Keep ahead, when the driveway turns down to the right, and cross a further field to a gate. From this gate firstly cross a ford, then go for a short distance along the right edge of a field. Pass through a gate in that edge and contour across the hillside to reach a gateway and stile at the lower edge of some woodland *[note – it may be somewhat boggy in this locality]*. Pass below the woodland and continue contouring to reach a wall stile. Climb over the stile then contour further, with a wall at a higher level to the left, and pass through a gate onto the metalled access drive to the property Swarthbank.

Ullswater from Auterstone

Ullswater Steamers. The Ullswater Navigation & Transit Co Ltd started operating steamer services in 1859, carrying mail, provisions and passengers around the lake. Of the several boats operating between Pooley Bridge, Howtown and Glenridding, 'Lady of the lake' was launched in 1877 and 'Raven' in 1889.

Howtown means 'the village by the hill'. The hill or 'how' in this case is thought to be nearby Hallin Fell.

Swarthbank Gill

6 Turn left for a few yards, along the drive. Pass between stone entrance pillars and immediately turn off right, through a gate and onto a narrow paved path that is parallel with the drive. Follow this path as it passes by Swarthbank, to emerge onto a turning area at the further side. Turn right and pass by a static caravan to a gate set at the further side. *[Note: this gate is somewhat hidden from view and should not be mistaken for a more prominent gate set in the higher wall of the property]* From the gate descend steeply across the diagonal of a field, to a gate in the further lower left corner. Pass through the gate onto the road and a boat launch ramp at Howtown and cross diagonally right to a gate on the further side of the ramp. From here continue alongside the shore of Ullswater to reach a footbridge close to Howtown pier which is served by the Ullswater Steamers service.

At this point the walk may be left to travel back to Pooley Bridge by boat, or it may be joined from the boat for the higher level route back to Pooley Bridge.

7 Cross the footbridge onto the lakeside path signed *Public footpath · Sandwick*. Continue beside the shore to reach a metalled driveway after passing through the second of two gates. Turn left, away from the lake, along the driveway and through a gate to a junction with the Howtown to Pooley Bridge road. Cross over and follow another metalled access, firstly past the Howtown Hotel then between dwellings. Continue uphill to the right side of Fusedale Beck, to a cattle grid and gate where the access road reaches open countryside. From the cattle grid turn left, off the access road and cross a stone footbridge over the Beck. Turn left, off the bridge and continue along then gently uphill on a broad section of enclosed path to reach a gate near the property 'Mellguards'. Turn right and uphill, from the gate and pass by the property to a further gate that leads onto open fellside.

8 Once through the gate the route commences its traverse, along the fellside and above the enclosed fields, back to Pooley Bridge. Proceed along the path with a wall on the immediate left side. Pass by the Outward Bound's Howtown residential centre (built in 2007/8), then Swarthbank. The path then rises gently and steadily, with the wall on the immediate left side. After about a mile from Mellguards a signed bridleway leaves through a gate to the left. Pass by the gate and bridleway route and keep the wall on the left. Cross a ford and shortly after, a footbridge over Swarthbeck Gill.

Continue and cross a second ford, then after a further half mile the path comes alongside Auterstone Wood before reaching a junction of paths, with low level direction signage. At this point the wall veers away to the left

9 **Leave the junction by the right hand path** which is signed *Moor Divick · Helton*. Proceed steeply uphill on Lock Bank, below the crags of Barton Fell, with ever improving panoramic views of Ullswater. After about two thirds of a mile of steady climbing the path flattens out beside the wall corner of a woodland area known as Barton Park. From here continue ahead, with a wall now to the left side and after a further third of a mile reach the steeply sided gully of Aik Beck. A sign indicating *Pooley Bridge 1¾m* will be passed at this point. Turn with the path to the right and drop down to ford Aik Beck. Proceed uphill, away from the Beck and continue ahead on a broad path that crosses a low hillside. Ignore lesser paths to right and left and follow the path (sometimes gravelly, sometimes broad and grassy) as it gently crosses open land before dropping noticeably as a rough stony path to cross a ford. Once over the ford rise up a little. To the right will be the ancient stone circle called 'The Cockpit'.

10 **Turn left through 90° with the path,** on leaving the stone circle and continue for a further third of a mile to a junction of paths on the hillside, beside a large stone cairn. Turn left at the junction and continue downhill on a broad stony track to reach a gate at Roehead at the head of a metalled road. From Roehead follow the road downhill, past several wayside seats, for about half a mile, to reach a junction with the road to Howtown. Cross over this junction and continue past houses, a church and another road junction (with the B5320 road), to reach the centre of Pooley Bridge and the end of the walk.

The Cockpit is the largest of several stone circles on Askham Fell. It is thought that the stone circle is from the Bronze Age and that it may have had a settlement connected with it. The stone circle has an internal diameter of 85 ft. Some of the stones are more than a metre in height.

Aik Beck ford

A walk around and to the summit of one of Lakeland's most popular hills with panoramic views of Ullswater and the eastern fells

FACTFILE

Distance
4.7 miles (7.5km)
Cumulative height: 1350 ft
Our rating: Moderate

Getting there
Regular scheduled boat service from Pooley Bridge or Glenridding to and from Howtown pier. Parking in the car park at the top of the hause by St Peter's church between Howtown and Martindale.

Local services
Seasonal hotel in Howtown; shops, public houses and cafés in Pooley Bridge.

Start grid NY435192
If travelling by boat NY443198

Map
OS Explorer OL5, English Lakes north-eastern area

The walk begins at the hause between Howtown and Martindale, by St Peter's Church. It then descends to Howtown, at the foot of Fusedale and the boat pier (an alternative start). The route then circles Hallin Fell and follows the shore path to Sandwick and field paths back to the hause. A steep climb up to the summit of the Fell is then followed by a high level panoramic route and descent back again to the hause. Good views can be gained from the walk of Ullswater, Martindale and Boredale, together with many of the eastern Lakeland fells.

The Walk

1 With your back to the road and Hallin Fell commence the walk across the rough parking area with the entrance to St Peter's church to your left. At the back of the car park continue steeply uphill ahead, onto the top of a low rocky mound. Pass across the mound then descend and veer left to join a wide path on the flank of the hillside. This path leads downhill to the right side of Howtown, which can be seen ahead. Follow this path, with fine views of Howtown Bay and eventually, with a wall on the immediate left side, drop steeply down to reach a concrete farm access road.

Scale: 4cm = 1km (0.6 mile)

2 Turn left, along the access road. Cross a cattle grid and descend downhill for about 250 yards, to reach a junction amongst buildings. Turn right, with a building on the immediate left side, then continue ahead onto a grassy path. Follow this path, with Fusedale Beck on the immediate right and a fence on the left to shortly pass through a gate onto the local road at Howtown. Turn right, along the road and upon reaching a turning area and boat launch ramp on the left, turn left and through a gate at the side of the ramp onto a lakeside path beside Ullswater. Follow this path for a short distance to reach a footbridge. Don't cross over the footbridge at this time but veer right along the boat landing jetty for a view of Ullswater (Howtown Wyke).

[Note: For boat passengers follow the walk description from here.]

3 Pass along the boat landing jetty then turn right, across a footbridge, onto a lakeside path signed *Sandwick*. Proceed along a level path amongst trees, with a fence on the left side and the lakeshore on the immediate right. After passing through two gates reach a metalled access road leading to the property 'Waternook'. Continue in the same direction for a short distance along this access road then turn off left through a gate. Follow a path, away from the lakeside and ascend a series of hillside steps between trees to reach a further gate. Once through the gate turn right onto a contouring path set above a wall on the lower slopes of Hallin Fell. Proceed along this path as it meanders a little above pastureland, with the wall on the immediate right side and views of Howtown Bay and Ullswater. Pass by the end of the wall, then a seat and descend over a rocky section to reach Geordie's Crag where the path begins a turn through about 90°. At this point panoramic views can be gained along Ullswater towards its eastern end at Pooley Bridge.

St Peter's Church

Howtown as a settlement dates from the 17th Century. The name is derived from 'the village by the hill (how(e))', the hill being Hallin Fell, which is characteristically compact, free-standing and relatively steep sided.

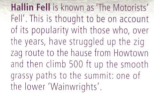

Hallin Fell is known as 'The Motorists' Fell'. This is thought to be on account of its popularity with those who, over the years, have struggled up the zig zag route to the hause from Howtown and then climb 500 ft up the smooth grassy paths to the summit: one of the lower 'Wainwrights'.

Martindale

4 Complete the turn and proceed along a rocky path. Descend steeply at one point, pass through bracken and cross several small gills. Rise up a little after nearing the lake shore to reach a gate at a wall and fence boundary to Hallinhag Wood. Once in the woodland continue ahead on an undulating path within sight of the lake shore. At times cross myriads of tree roots. Follow this path as it meanders through the woodland for about three quarters of a mile and eventually descend near the edge of the woodland to reach a further gate. Pass through this gate, then out of the woodland immediately alongside the lake shore at Sandwick Bay. Veer left, as waymarked, pass through a gate and proceed uphill across meadows. Pass through three further gates to emerge on a ledge type path that descends towards Sandwick. At the foot of the descent veer left with the path into a beck side meadow and within a short distance turn around to the right. Cross a bridge over Sandwick Beck and pass through a gate onto the turning circle at Sandwick road end.

5 Turn left, uphill at first, along the road for a little over a quarter of a mile. At a junction with a metalled access road turn off left, across a bridge over Boredale Beck. At a track junction signed *Footpath: Howtown,* turn left, through a gate and cross a bridge over Sandwick Beck. Turn right, immediately after the bridge and climb over a stile, again signed *Howtown,* onto a beck side path. Pass beside the property 'Bridge End' and through a gate into a field. From the gate veer left and uphill along a hillside path that gradually turns to the right, to reach a further gate that leads into the property, 'Hallin Bank'. Pass through this property and a further gate on the far side. Continue ahead (not along a track) onto a narrow hillside path to reach a set of steps that lead up to a gate. Once through the gate contour across a hillside meadow to reach a small gate on the far side. Climb down steps from the gate and veer right, across the next meadow, to a stile set beside a gate. From this stile the climb of Hallin Fell begins.

[Note: If the climb is not being tackled continue ahead to shortly reach the car park by St Peter's Church, where the walk began.]

6 The climb of Hallin Fell. Once over the stile veer immediately left and uphill onto a rising grassy path. Keep a wall to the left side and at a sharp left wall corner turn left onto a wider steep path. Continue uphill along a wide grassy path between bracken, with the wall again on the left side. When the wall turns away to the left continue ahead, still rising steeply. The path veers a little to the left and makes towards a lower point between two higher level prominent rocky outcrops. Upon arrival between the outcrops continue on the path as it turns around to the right. The summit obelisk/cairn will then be in view and a further slight rise is required to reach the summit at 1271 ft.

7 Pass across the summit, and face towards the straight length of Ullswater that leads north-eastwards towards Pooley Bridge in the distance. Drop down a little, along a grassy path and cross over a slight mound to reach a path junction. Take the left path at this junction which leads into a grassy trough that descends between buttresses, again towards the length of Ullswater. Follow this path downhill as far as a grassy path junction amongst bracken (with an exposed rock in the centre), immediately past the point where the right buttress falls away. Continue along the right path which then curves around to the right and passes below the buttress and onto a gently undulating portion of upper hillside. Veer right at a main path junction and shortly after join a further grassy path that has come down from the side of the buttress. Continue then ahead and over the lip at the edge of the undulating section of hillside. At this point the car park and St Peter's Church will be visible ahead down slanting paths. Continue steeply downhill using one of the grassy path routes that lead to the hause between Howtown and Martindale and the end of the walk.

[Note: If you started the walk at the Howtown ferry landing jetty cross over the road at the hause onto the car park area beside St Peter's Church. From there follow the walk guidance given in paragraphs 1 and 2 to return to the jetty. The same guidance should be followed by boat passengers who haven't climbed up Hallin Fell, who arrived at the hause directly from guidance in paragraph 5.]

Steel Knotts from Hallin Fell

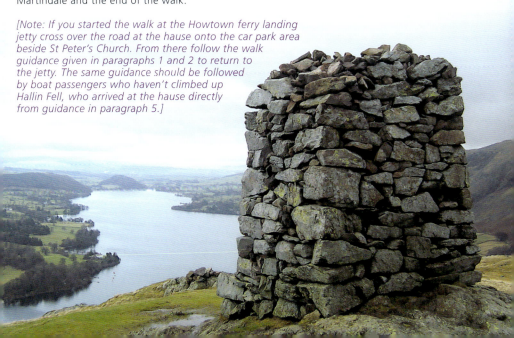

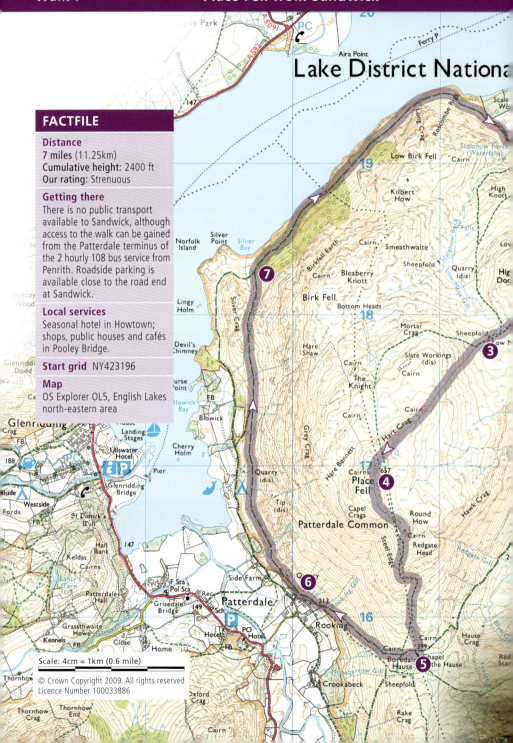

FACTFILE

Distance
7 miles (11.25km)
Cumulative height: 2400 ft
Our rating: Strenuous

Getting there
There is no public transport available to Sandwick, although access to the walk can be gained from the Patterdale terminus of the 2 hourly 108 bus service from Penrith. Roadside parking is available close to the road end at Sandwick.

Local services
Seasonal hotel in Howtown; shops, public houses and cafés in Pooley Bridge.

Start grid   NY423196

Map
OS Explorer OL5, English Lakes north-eastern area

Scale: 4cm = 1km (0.6 mile)

Explore an iconic Lakeland Fell and its surrounds. Return by the side of Ullswater along the path described by Alfred Wainwright as 'the most beautiful and rewarding walk in Lakeland'

The walk begins at Sandwick road end. It climbs up the slopes of Sleet Fell on the west side of Boredale then up higher onto Hart Crag and Place Fell Summit. It then descends to Boredale Hause and the Patterdale area, before traversing the lower slopes of Place Fell alongside Ullswater. The walk boasts a series of splendid high level views of the eastern and central Lakeland fells. Opportunities exist on clear days for 'aerial' type views over Patterdale and Glenridding from the summit area of Place Fell.

The walk can commence and finish at the 108 bus terminus in Patterdale, where 'pay and display' car parking facilities also exist. The additional half mile of route description to reach the walk is included at the end of paragraph 5.

Sleet Fell and Hallin Fell

The Walk

1 Commence the walk uphill along the road, away from the turning area. At the top of the first rise the wall on the left veers away from the road at the driveway entrance to a property named 'Mill Howe'. At this point turn off the road to the right and proceed quite steeply uphill, along a grassy path through bracken. Keep on this path as it rises and gradually turns towards the left to reach the outside of a field wall corner. Pass by the corner and gently drop downhill for a while with the wall on the immediate left side. After about a quarter of a mile the path levels out a little as it gently rounds a corner to the right. In this vicinity there is a path junction with a faint path keeping close to the wall and the major, clearer path veering right to begin a steep climb up the side of Sleet Fell.

2 Continue along the steeper path as it rises across the slope of Sleet Fell on the west side of Boredale. (Boredale: the valley with the store house) The path rises fairly consistently across the slope, by about 500ft in half a mile. Views during this traverse become increasingly stunning and widespread. The path then turns somewhat, into the hillside, and contains some short very steep sections. It then reaches a junction with a more prominent grassy hilltop path. At this point turn left, onto the path and proceed up and around the shoulder of High Dodd. (High Dodd: the high, compact, rounded hill) Once over the shoulder the path then descends slightly as it crosses the somewhat spongy area of Low Moss to reach a path junction and ruined sheepfold at the head of Low Moss Gill.

Place Fell summit

3 Pass to the left side of the sheep fold then proceed steeply uphill on a partially eroded groove path to reach a rocky cairn after a short steep scramble. This is at the highest point in the immediate view when climbing up. Pass by the cairn onto a rocky ridge route on Hart Crag and continue ahead, winding between rocks and past small tarns. The triangulation pillar of Place Fell summit will come into view. Follow a suitable scramble route to the summit of the mountain in the vicinity of the pillar.

Hart Crag means the rocky height frequented by the hart or stag.

4 Turn sharp left from the direction in which you approached the summit, descend down rocks and proceed across terrain between small tarns towards the lower second summit of Round How. Turn right, off this second summit, and descend steeply to gain the main downward path which leads south towards Boredale Hause.

[Note: The initial descent from Round How is a steep rock scramble. To avoid the scramble retrace your steps back a few yards from Round How, towards Place Fell summit, then turn left along a path that contours around to meet the main path below the scramble area.]

Continue steeply downhill on a clear path, winding a little on the hillside. Parts of this path are stepped and others have a steep loose gravel surface. As the slope shallows out a cross junction of paths is reached, just in front of a ruin at Boredale Hause.

Place Fell. 2154ft high (the mountain with open, level areas). The Fell is described by Wainwright in the following terms: "Few fells are so well favoured as Place Fell for appraising neighbouring heights. It occupies an exceptionally good position in the curve of Ullswater, in the centre of a great bowl of hills; its summit commands a very beautiful and impressive panorama. Place Fell should be an early objective, for no other viewpoint gives such an appreciation of the design of this lovely corner of Lakeland."

Round How means the hill with the circular top.

Place Fell from High Dodd

5 Turn right at this junction and proceed steeply downhill on a path that descends (slanting down the hillside) towards Patterdale and Ullswater. After descending a little way the path zig zags to join a second. It then continues downhill as the upper of two rather stony parallel hillside paths. Close to the foot of the hillside the two paths join, just above the hamlet of Rooking. After a further 200 yards a path junction is reached. Here the main route descends steeply to the left towards the hamlet and a lesser path keeps ahead and uphill. Continue along this lesser upward path.

[Note: This is the point in the walk where the route can be joined, if you start and finish at the 108 bus terminus in Patterdale. After leaving the bus continue along the main road in the same direction that the bus has travelled. Pass through the central part of Patterdale village, where the road narrows between buildings. Turn off left, after a further 200 yards, along a local metalled access road leading over the river and across the valley to Rooking. Turn right at the road end (after a quarter of a mile) and pass through a gate. Rise up steeply for a few yards and once clear of dwellings keep uphill a little further to reach the upward path of the walk and turn left. (you will be able to leave the walk again later at this point to return to the bus terminus)]

6 Follow the path uphill to reach an area of former slate quarry workings. Pass across these, generally keeping to the upper level path. After passing through the first set of quarry workings the path reaches a junction, beside a small hillock to the left. Turn right here and uphill, along a stony path and cross further former quarry workings. From this point the path begins to contour, with panoramic views across Ullswater to Patterdale and Glenridding. Ahead will be seen Silver Crag, where the path rises to a low hause to the right side.

A glimpse of Brotherswater on the descent from Place Fell.

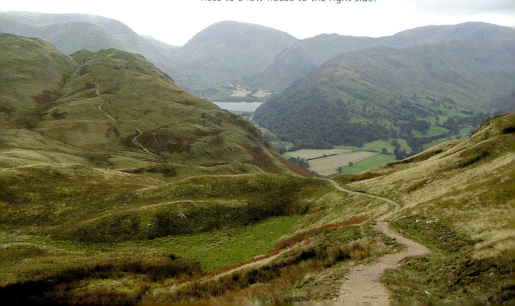

Silver Crag Hause

En route to the hause a path junction will be reached where the right path rises steeply and the left drops down gently. Take the left path at this point, as the right leads up to the top of Place Fell. Pass across the hause beside Silver Crag, then descend quite steeply along a stony, but partly stepped path that passes through low juniper woodland, to reach a path junction by Silver Bay.

7 Turn right and continue along the stony path that passes through woodland close to the shore of Ullswater. Ullswater is the second largest of the English Lakes at seven and a half miles in length and, on average, three quarters of a mile wide. The Lake is considered by many to be the most attractive and unspoilt, especially because of its setting with the curving shoreline fields and woodlands which give way to rock faces and vistas of mountain grandeur. This path is very clear to follow but is somewhat undulating and requires care, due to rock outcrops and tree roots. In places there are good viewpoints across Ullswater. After about one and a half miles the path moves away from the shore area and is separated from Ullswater by enclosed woodland and fields. Once the enclosed area is reached keep the wall to the left side for the remaining three quarters of a mile to Sandwick. In this section of the route a footbridge will be crossed, over Scalehow Beck. A little later a shallow gill leading down from Sleet Fell will need to be forded. The path eventually reaches Sandwick and drops down to the road end and the finishing point for the walk.

The Ullswater Steamer en route to Glenridding.

[Note: If you have commenced the walk from the bus terminus at Patterdale continue by following the descriptions in paragraphs 1 to 5, to return to your starting point.]

Ullswater panorama: a classic lakeside mountain and the excitement of Aira Force.

FACTFILE

Distance
4 miles (6.5km)
Cumulative height: 1200 ft
Our rating: Moderate

Getting there
Regular public transport from Penrith or Glenridding (Bus route 108). Summer service from Keswick. Parking in Aira Force National Trust car park for which there is a charge for non-Trust members.

Local services
Café close to Aira Force car park; refreshments also available in Pooley Bridge, Dockray & Glenridding.

Start grid NY400200

Map
OS Explorer OL5, English Lakes north-eastern area

The walk begins at Aira Force car park, close to the shores of Ullswater and about 10 miles to the west of Penrith.

The walk benefits from the panoramic views that can be gained along the path that traverses the south and east flanks of Gowbarrow. It then gains the summit of the mountain before traversing the upper levels to reach a grandstand view over Ullswater and beyond from Green Hill. Upon return it explores the area around Aira Force waterfall.

The Walk

1 Commence the walk within the car park. With your back to the car park entrance and A592 road proceed along the left circulatory road. Pass a sign indicating *To Waterfalls*, to reach the pedestrian exit gateway at the rear, alongside a set of local interest display boards. Pass through the gateway and proceed along a stone surfaced path with woodland to the right side. Once through a gate continue along the path for a further 400ft to reach a gate that leads into the woodland area associated with Aira Force. From the gate proceed a short distance along a woodland path, veer right at a path junction then drop down to and cross a bridge over Aira Beck.

Scale: 4cm = 1km (0.6 mile)

Lyulf's or Lyulph's Tower was built in 1780 by the Duke of Norfolk as a gothic folly styled hunting seat. The castellated building forms three sides of an octagon, with four hexagonal towers and round arched windows.

2 From the bridge continue ahead, then up some steps. Keep right at a path junction and a little later right again, to reach a stile at the edge of the woodland. Once over, continue to a path junction, then veer right, along the foot of the hillside. To the right the back of 'Lyulph's Tower' will be visible. After a further 200 yards the path splits, with one route continuing along the contour and the other climbing steeply up the flank of Gowbarrow.

3 Proceed along the steeper rising path, which, upon the easing of the gradient becomes one of Lakeland's more stunning panoramic paths. After about half a mile the path rounds a bend, passes a stone memorial seat (dated October 1905) and splits close to a stile in the right fence that leads to the cairn on the top of Yew Crag.

The name **Gowbarrow** means 'the breezy hill'. The area of Gowbarrow Park roughly corresponds to the Fell. This was a mediaeval deer park of about 2000 acres which was stocked with up to 700 head of fallow deer.

Gowbarrow from Sandwick

The view from **Yew Crag** is considered to be one of the best in the Lake District. The Cairn lies at an elevation of about 525ft above Ullswater and has commanding views along the full length of Ullswater and to the mountains beyond: both in the Lake District and the North Pennines across the Eden valley.

4 Visit the cairn and viewpoint then return to the path junction and continue uphill on the left path along a short rocky section of path. The route turns generally from the southern to the eastern flank of Gowbarrow and continues to contour, with slight rises and falls. After about three quarters of a mile from the cairn the route crosses a footbridge across a steep ravine in the hillside, then drops down quite steeply to reach a path junction beside the ruins of a former stone shooting lodge. Turn left at this junction, then continue gradually uphill with a gill and wall beyond to the right side. The path may be a little boggy in places. Where a stile becomes visible in the wall corner to the right, veer around to the left with the path. Climb up more steeply towards the summit of Gowbarrow Fell which will be visible ahead. The path skirts the right side of the summit crag before turning back and up to reach the top of the mountain. A triangulation pillar, which incorporates a National Trust plaque, marks the summit of Gowbarrow (1579ft/481m).

5 Upon leaving the summit a path should first be located that leads away to the south, through heather, across the hilltops of Gowbarrow Park. When looking in that direction it will be noted that the path first passes over the left flank of a lower, nearer, summit which contains a notable upstanding rock. Drop down the summit crag, cross a small depression then proceed along the path to the south and across the shoulder of the next lower summit area. Keep then ahead and shortly reach the top of a short but steeper craggy descent.

Gowbarrow summit

Drop down then continue along a grassy path that winds its way across the undulating summit area of the Park in the general direction of Place Fell (which is on the further side of Ullswater), which should be visible in the middle distance. Paths will lead away to left and right but from each junction keep along the path that retains the most height to eventually reach the summit cairn of Green Hill. Pass over to a further lower grassy hillock that provides a dramatic panoramic view of Ullswater, Place Fell and other mountains beyond, atop a steep slope that leads down to the lake.

6 Turn right at this point and locate a grassy path that leads in a westerly direction down towards the woodland around Aira Force. Continue along this path, which will link with others from across Gowbarrow Park. It will descend quite steeply, parallel with Ullswater, keeping in the main its grassy base. This path passes beside Bernard Pike, then drops down through bracken, with some zig zagging. It eventually reaches a cross path then a stile at the edge of the Aira Force woodland. Climb over the stile and continue ahead through the trees to shortly reach some slab rocks, a path junction and the bridge at the top level of Aira Force.

7 Cross the bridge, viewing the falls en route, then up steps to reach a junction with a path from the right. Keep ahead, then turn around to the left on the path to reach a further junction where a stepped path descends to the left. Pass down the steps to reach the bottom of Aira Force and a second lower bridge. Again view the falls, cross over the bridge then continue along the path with the Aira Beck to the right side. This path leads along the valley, climbing up a little before reaching a junction with the outward route of this walk. From this junction descend the steps then cross over the Aira Beck once again. Retrace the route back to the Aira Force car park and the end of the walk.

The **Aira Beck** flows over a number of waterfalls within the National Trust woodland area. This includes the main 70ft Aira Force. Both the higher and lower bridges provide good viewing positions for Aira Force. The lower bridge was erected in memory of Cecil Spring Rice (1859-1919) UK Ambassador to the US during the Great War and author of the hymn 'I vow to thee my country'. The upper in memory of his brother Stephen Edward Spring Rice (1856-1902), a Principal Clerk at HM Treasury. Both brothers lived at Old Church, Ullswater.

Green Hill

Aira Force, High Force and a dramatic high level traverse to view the classic Ullswater and Glencoyne panorama

The walk begins at Aira Force car park, close to the shores of Ullswater and about 10 miles to the west of Penrith. The first part of the walk explores the valley of the Aira Beck taking in Aira Force, the Aira ravine and High Force, together with Dockray. It then climbs up steeply onto Watermillock Common to gain the fellside path which provides high level panoramic views of Ullswater and the eastern Lakes. On the return the walk descends through Glencoyne Park and visits the lower level area of Aira Force

FACTFILE

Distance
5.3 miles (8.5km)
Cumulative height: 1400 ft
Our rating: Strenuous

Getting there
Regular public transport from Penrith or Glenridding (Bus route 108). Summer service from Keswick. Parking in Aira Force National Trust car park for which there is a charge for non-Trust members.

Local services
Café close to Aira Force car park; refreshments also available in Pooley Bridge, Dockray & Glenridding.

Start grid NY400200

Map
OS Explorer OL5, English Lakes north-eastern area

The land in the vicinity of **Aira Beck** was laid out with paths in the 1860s and planted with conifers as a pleasure garden for nearby Lyulph's Tower: a hunting lodge of the Howards of Greystoke castle

Scale: 4cm = 1km (0.6 mile)

The Walk

1 Commence the walk within the car park. With your back to the car park entrance and A592 road proceed along the left circulatory road. Pass a sign indicating *To Waterfalls*, to reach the pedestrian exit gateway at the rear, alongside a set of local interest display boards. Pass through the gateway and proceed along a stone surfaced path with woodland to the right side. Once through a gate continue along the path for a further 400 yds. to reach a gate that leads into the woodland area associated with Aira Force. From the gate proceed a short distance along a woodland path, veer right at a path junction then drop down and cross a footbridge over Aira Beck.

2 Continue ahead from the bridge and up some steps. Keep right at a path junction, up more steps, then a little later bear left at a second junction. Upon reaching a third path junction bear down left on the lesser path and shortly cross over rocks and various paths to reach the upper Aira Force footbridge. Cross over the bridge and up some steps the other side. At the top turn sharp right and pass through a gate onto a beck side path. Follow this path as it rises gradually through the woodland, with Aira Beck to the right side. Keep left at a path junction, then drop down from the top of the rise to reach another footbridge that crosses over the chasm part of Aira Beck.

3 Once over the footbridge climb up a rocky outcrop then proceed ahead, with Aira Beck now to the left side. The path shortly turns up to the right to meet another higher path within the woodland. Turn left onto the higher path and continue uphill along a fairly rocky path. Pass beside the High Force waterfall and eventually reach a gateway. This gateway marks the edge of the Gowbarrow Park National Trust land holding.

The **Aira Beck** flows over a number of waterfalls within the National Trust woodland area. This includes the main 70ft Aira Force. Both the higher and lower bridges provide good viewing positions for Aira Force. The lower bridge was erected in memory of Cecil Spring Rice (1859-1919) UK Ambassador to the US during the Great War and author of the hymn 'I vow to thee my country'. The upper in memory of his brother Stephen Edward Spring Rice (1856-1902), a Principal Clerk at HM Treasury. Both brothers lived at Old Church, Ullswater.

Dockray means the 'nook in the hollow'

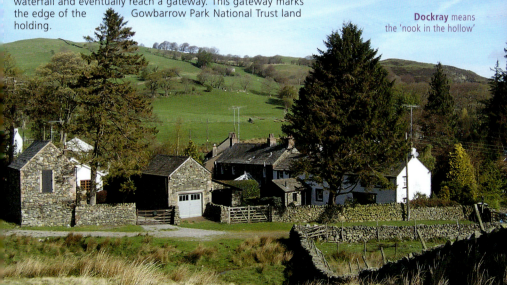

Pass through then continue uphill through a further section of woodland. Cross a ford and pass through a gate onto open pasture, then continue across a shallow hillside shoulder area to reach a further gate close to a sign directing to **Dockray and Ulcatrow**. Once through the gate ford a stream, then continue downhill along a track to shortly reach a junction of tracks. Bear left at the junction, signed to Dockray, pass through a gate (adjoining stile), cross a bridge and continue on a track past the property *'Millses'*. Keep uphill, pass through a further gate then, with the track now enclosed, pass by various properties to reach another gate and the A5091 road at Dockray.

4 **Turn left,** along the road, then keep along the side of the road signed to *Patterdale* and *Ullswater* at the road junction. Cross a bridge over Aira Beck and shortly turn off to the right along an access road signed as a *Public Footpath*. Once through the gate at the head of the access turn sharp left and cross a small watercourse onto open hillside. Keep a wall to the left at first then, when it turns away to the left, keep ahead and uphill along a narrow grassy path. Upon shortly approaching the steeper slopes of Bracken How veer around to the right and continue along a contouring route. Keep ahead at a grassy path junction and cross a first ford. Continue to a second ford (of Pounder Sike) and once over veer left at a path junction. Commence a steady uphill climb onto Watermillock Common. The path leads towards the left shoulder of the Common and in places has some steeper sections as it winds around and across rock outcrops. It is also boggy in places. As the path rises, the wall that separates Watermillock Common from Glencoyne Park will come into view to the left side. At the head of the first section of climbing the path will come immediately alongside this wall. The route of the path now contours beside the wall, with panoramic views down and across Ullswater. It then rises up once again between the wall and the crags of Swineside Knott and around a wall bend. Another section of contouring is encountered and a wooden stile will eventually come into view which is set in the wall to the left. Make down, where convenient, to climb over the stile. *[Note: The route of the walk turns quite sharply at this point to return towards Aira Force.]*

High Force

5 Once over the stile turn to the left onto a steep downward path. This path leads into and through Glencoyne Park. The route at first is grassy, but steep, passing through hillside bracken. It then traverses a section of mature woodland to reach a stile. From the stile, for a distance of about a mile, the path continues to descend in an undulating and winding manner, with several boggy sections to negotiate and gills to cross. The route is clear but given the splendid views and scenery, it is probably advisable to amble along this path and enjoy all it has to offer. It eventually reaches a stile that leads onto the A5091 road.

6 From the stile cross over the road and into the higher car park for Aira Force. Bear right from the entrance to the car park to the start of the footpath that leads down to Aira Force. Continue downhill through trees along this path to reach a gate at the further woodland edge. Once through, bear right and downhill, crossing a footbridge to reach a gate. Pass through the gate and turn left, then opposite a seat turn right onto a stepped path. Pass down the steps to reach the bottom of Aira Force and the lower bridge across Aira Beck. View the falls, cross over the bridge then continue along the path with Aira Beck to the right side. This path leads along the valley, climbing up a little before reaching a junction with the outward route of the walk. From this junction descend the steps then cross over the Aira Beck once again. Retrace the route back to the Aira Force car park and the end of the walk.

Glencoyne: the 'reedy valley' or 'beautiful valley'. The panoramic views at this location offer dramatic, high level vistas of Ullswater and its surrounds. The impact of these can be accentuated through the ever changing weather effects in and around the valley.

A short walk with alternative options to go around or over this wooded hill

View from Dunmallard

Scale: 500m (0.3 mile)

The walk (which has two options) starts from the entrance to the car park on the north-west bank of the River Eamont, alongside the B5320 road. This is just across the bridge from the village.

Option A: An easy circular walk around the lower flanks of the hill.

Option B: A more strenuous 'figure of eight' shaped walk to the hill top fort followed by field paths and a riverside path beside the River Eamont.

Both options commence at the same point along a common section of route and finish back at the car park entrance.

Walk A

A1 From the car park entrance pass through a kissing gate into the woodland and turn right onto a path signed *Public Footpath* to *Dacre*. Proceed along this path, rising gently, then more steeply up the lower flank of Dunmallard Hill. The path levels out close to the right edge of the woodland and reaches a cross junction of paths with a low level direction finger post on the right side.

FACTFILE

Distance
Option A: 1 mile (1.6km)
Our rating: Easy
Option B: 1.5 miles (2.4km)
Our Rating: Easy

Getting there
Regular public transport from Penrith (Bus route 108) or boat from Glenridding or Howtown. Car park and roadside parking in and around Pooley Bridge.

Local services
Shops, cafés and public houses in village.

Start grid NY469244

Map
OS Explorer OL5, English Lakes north-eastern area

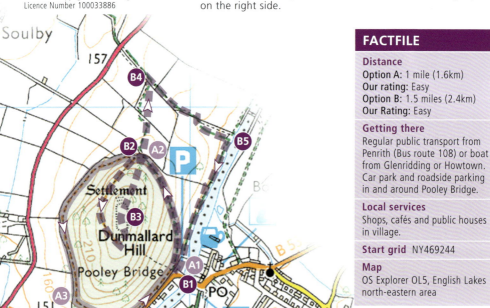

A2 **Cross this junction** and after a further 20 or so yards veer right at another path junction onto a downward sloping path. Continue along this path as it meanders close to the right edge of the woodland, with fields visible beyond. The path provides some good views in places, out of the woodland, of Ullswater and the nearby fells.

A3 **Where the fields end continue along the path** as it turns around to the left and descends quite steeply, deeper within the woodland. At a shallow junction join with a path that comes in from the right and continue ahead, again downhill. The path then comes close to the B5320 road and houses at the entrance to Pooley Bridge village. Continue, with the road close by on the right, to once again reach the initial kissing gate and car park entrance and the end of the walk.

Walk B

B1 **From the car park entrance pass through a kissing gate** into the woodland and turn right onto a path signed *Public Footpath* to *Dacre*. Proceed along this path, rising gently, then more steeply up the lower flank of Dunmallard Hill. The path levels out close to the right edge of the woodland and reaches a cross junction of paths with a low level direction finger post on the right side.

Dunmallard (or Dunmallet) is the wooded hill, possessing an ancient hill fort, which overlooks Pooley Bridge at the northern end of Ullswater.

The walk is a good woodland walk but only brief glimpses can be gained of the surrounding hills, even at the summit. These are better during winter months after the deciduous trees have shed their leaves. There have clearly been viewpoints in former years but these have now become obscured by foliage. The section of the walk outside the woodland enables the grandeur of the area to be better appreciated.

Approaching Dunmallard

B2 Cross this junction and after a further 20 or so yards veer left at another path junction onto a gently rising path. Continue along this path as it spirals up the higher slope of the hill, eventually levelling out at another junction on the further side of the hill. Veer left at this junction then turn sharply left off this path and follow a faint path up the short, steep slope which forms the outer mound of the former hill top fort. *[Note: There are three paths of differing steepness up the slope in this vicinity.]*

B3 Once up the slope continue ahead to the Dunmallard summit. Cross over the wooded summit then descend down a fairly steep narrow path ahead to reach, once again, the cross junction of paths by the woodland edge. Pass over this junction again and leave the woodland through a kissing gate into a sloping meadow, along a path signed to *Dacre*. Cross the meadow to a wooden stile, then a further meadow to a second stile.

View down the Eamont to Pooley Bridge from the bottom of Dunmallard Hill (walk B)

B4 After this stile turn sharply right and keep along the right side of a field. Pass by an unused stile then a field gate to reach a gate (and stile) set in the fence on the right. Pass through this gate, then continue downhill to reach the bank of the River Eamont.

B5 Once the river bank is reached turn right, along the riverside path. Pass through a further gate back into woodland, then continue past a number of riverside seats to reach the car park beside Pooley Bridge and the end of the walk.

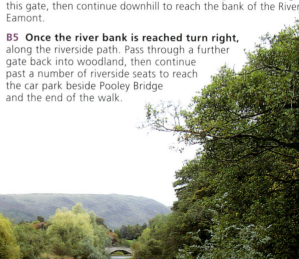

Walking
in the
Lowther Valley

ramblers
at the heart of walking

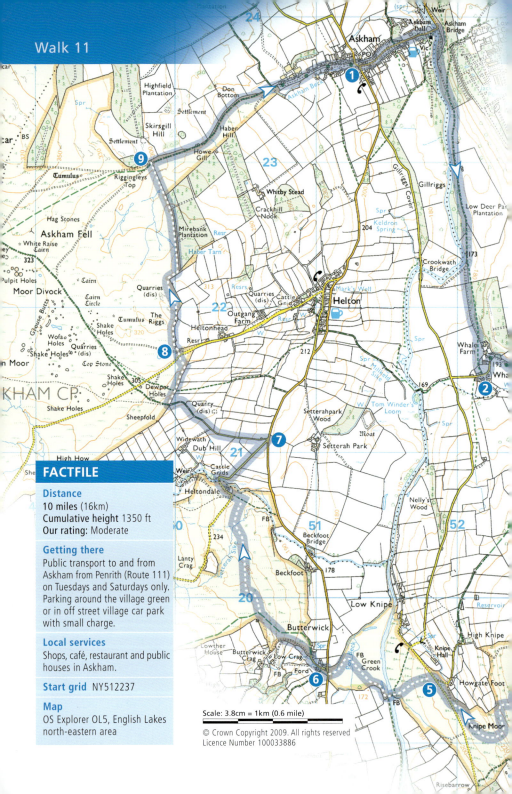

Walk 11

Scale: 3.8cm = 1km (0.6 mile)

FACTFILE

Distance
10 miles (16km)
Cumulative height 1350 ft
Our rating: Moderate

Getting there
Public transport to and from
Askham from Penrith (Route 111)
on Tuesdays and Saturdays only.
Parking around the village green
or in off street village car park
with small charge.

Local services
Shops, café, restaurant and public
houses in Askham.

Start grid NY512237

Map
OS Explorer OL5, English Lakes
north-eastern area

A walk through
Lowther Park
and Valley with a
prominent viewpoint
of the eastern
Lakeland fells
and open access
moorland.

The walk begins at the main cross roads junction in Askham beside the Village Stores. It descends through the lower part of the village to the bridge over the River Lowther. It then traverses the southern part of Lowther Park rising up to and through 'The Squadrons' stands of trees. It turns to traverse upper levels of the Knipe Scar escarpment before descending steeply and crossing the Lowther Valley to Butterwick. The return to Askham is across open access land in Heltondale and higher up on Askham Fell.

Askham Bridge

The Walk

1 Commence the walk along the road, signed *Lowther 2 miles*, that leads gently downhill across the lower portion of Askham village green. Pass by dwellings and the Punchbowl Inn then drop down more steeply past St Peter's Church and across the bridge over the River Lowther. Once over turn immediately right, off the road, onto a woodland footpath. Keep right at a junction that occurs after a few yards and continue along the path above the river bank. After about a third of a mile from the bridge and following a shallow junction with a grassy track from the left, a gate is reached at the woodland edge. From the gate continue ahead along a wide track. The track descends gently at first and after passing through a gate continues alongside woodland to a further gate. Continue then straight ahead, ignore the track that follows the river as it turns sharply to the right and shortly after reach the gate at the lower corner of the wood ahead. From the gate continue gently uphill through the bottom of the wood. After about 400 yards, on the approach to a further farmyard gate, turn off right and climb over a stile, out of the wood, into a field. Bear left from the stile, with farm buildings to the left side. Pass through a gate at the field edge, then continue ahead across the next field to reach a gate atop a short flight of stone steps. Go through the gate, and follow a grassy enclosed path and out through a gateway beside a dwelling, onto the metalled country road at Whale hamlet.

DEFRA Conservation Walks. The route of the walk from Whalemoor to Knipescar Common is a temporary Permissive Bridleway set down at the behest of the Department for Environment, Food and Rural Affairs as part of a farm conservation scheme.

'The Squadrons' are the three stands of beech trees at In Scar that are visible as landmarks over much of Eden. The trees were at one time mistaken for English troops by raiding Scots.

Knipe Scar, which overlooks Bampton and Bampton Grange is a very prominent landscape feature in the Lowther Valley. The scar is composed of Carboniferous Limestone. The word 'Knipe' comes from the Old Norse (gnipa) meaning 'jutting crag or rocky summit'.

2 Turn left, along the road, and follow it through a gate as it passes farm buildings and turns right over a cattle grid. After a second cattle grid, the road bears right and begins to ascend. From the road junction just after the third cattle grid continue ahead uphill keeping along the road, to reach the farmstead of Whalemoor and shortly after the property Whalemoor Head. Continue gently uphill on the estate road to a point, just across a cattle grid, where the metalled road turns sharply left. At the point of the turn the three iconic stands of mature beech trees, known as the 'Squadrons', will dominate the view ahead of the hillside 'In Scar'. Don't turn with the road but continue ahead at this point making towards the gap between the left hand and middle, stands of trees. Just to the left of the point where the road turns a grassy track rises gently uphill towards the gap. This track should be located and followed through and beyond the gap to eventually reach a gate on the further side of the tree stands.

3 From the gate continue ahead gently downhill keeping to the grassy track. Take note, however, of the wall and plantation away to the right and when the track comes level with the end of the plantation look out for a crossing point of paths. At this crossing point turn sharply right and make towards a path direction post then on to the plantation wall corner. Keep the wall close by to the right to reach a gate that leads on to Knipescar Common, which is Open Access Land. At this point there is a splendid view of the Haweswater Reservoir. Turn right, having passed through the gate, along a grassy track with a wall to the right and clumps of gorse to the left. Once past the gorse move gradually to the left as the track gently rises onto limestone upland and follow a route, away from the track, along the top of Knipe Scar with continuous panoramic views. After about three quarters of a mile from the gate the highest point of the scar is reached (1,122 ft or 342 metres) where, with a little observation a circular Ordnance Survey surveying base will be spotted in the ground.

4 **From the highest point** continue along a few paces then carefully descend to a small 'nick' in the limestone escarpment. At this point turn left and pass downhill through the nick. Once through, turn to the right and continue along a path, across the hillside, but keep immediately above the layer of gorse and bracken. At a point which is level with a lone stunted tree on the escarpment to the right turn sharp left onto a broad grassy path that descends the hillside through the bracken. Follow this path as it slants downhill and turns a few times to eventually reach the bottom of the slope in a shallow 'trough' area on Knipe Moor. Here the moor rises gently beyond and more distinct troughs can be seen to left and right. At this point curve around the trough to the right and keeping on higher ground follow the grassy path amongst low clumps of gorse to reach a metalled local road. Bear right, onto the road, to shortly reach a road junction with a stone and concrete milk loading platform alongside.

5 **Turn left off the road,** by the platform, onto a sloping grassy path. Follow this path downhill and at the bottom of the slope reach the River Lowther and a suspension bridge across the river. Pass over the bridge then turn right onto open grassy riverside grazing land. Proceed along a grassy path with a wall at first on the left side. Once the wall has turned, veer away along the path to reach a footbridge across Pow Beck. From the footbridge the hamlet of Butterwick will be seen ahead. Continue along the path that veers left from the bridge beside a low embankment. After about 200 yards a gate is reached that leads onto the Bampton to Askham road just to the left of Butterwick Bridge. Once through the gate turn right, along the road and cross over Butterwick Bridge to reach the road junction in the hamlet.

Open Access Land is land which has been designated by the Government under the Countryside and Rights of Way Act to permit a 'right to roam' for the public.

Suspension bridge over the River Lowther

6 Turn left at the road junction and pass through a gate along a metalled access road. Upon reaching the property 'Fell End', where the metalling finishes, turn left up a track signed as a Permissive Bridleway. Pass through a gate and continue along the track to the point where it veers left towards a gate in the wall. Turn off the track here to the right and follow a faint rising path with a steeper hillside on the left side. At the top of the rise a stone field barn comes into view on the left side. Before coming level with the field barn locate, then follow, a faint contouring path to the right. Once on this path gently veer left across the hillside and rise up to the top of a broad shoulder area, among gorse bushes. Turn right, when on the shoulder and proceed gently downhill along the shoulder in a northerly direction, parallel with the valley below to the right. When near the lower part of the shoulder various faint paths join to make up a grassy track that turns to the left to reach a ford of Setterah Sike. Cross the Sike near the ford, then veer right and follow a grassy path until a 'T' junction of such paths is reached close to Heltondale Beck. Turn left and shortly reach a local road near the isolated residential property 'Heltondale'. Continue along this road, passing by the property, to reach a cattle grid. From the grid cross the bridge over Heltondale Beck, turn with the road and rise up steeply. After a further 400 yards reach a junction with the Bampton to Askham road.

Heltondale

7 **Turn sharp left** at the road junction onto a farm access road signed for *Widewath Farm*. Follow this road gently, then more steeply, uphill. Pass by a public bridleway sign indicating *Askham Fell 1/4 mile*. Where the metalled road turns away left continue ahead along an unsurfaced enclosed track to reach a gate that leads on to Askham Fell. Once through the gate turn sharp right and follow a grassy path, parallel with the wall on the right. Pass by three fields then turn left with the path, away from the wall, at a point where two gates in the wall are located close together. Once turned, pick out a higher wall corner then continue uphill to reach the wall, after crossing a metalled fell access road. A grassy track is located immediately beside the wall corner.

Askham Fell is a very popular area for walkers with good access. The Fell is pepperpotted with ancient features including stone and cairn circles. It also exhibits several areas of limestone shake holes and Roman features associated with the route of the High Street Roman Road.

8 **Veer left at the wall corner,** along the grassy track and continue around the eastern edge of Askham Fell, with the wall on the right side. Pass by a former quarry area and where the track turns to enter a field keep ahead and round a further wall corner to the right. The boundary then turns left at another corner beside a pitted and fairly boggy area. Turn likewise and continue along the fell boundary, now with the Mirebank Plantation on the right side. The boundary with the plantation is about 600 yards long following which the path drops steeply down to cross the depression of the 'dry' course of Askham Beck. It then rises up steeply and after a further short distance reaches a gate, on the right, in the wall.

9 **Turn right** and pass through the gate then continue ahead gently downhill along a grassy track, with Askham village now visible. The track becomes stony and in places may be wet as it approaches Askham. After about two thirds of a mile from the gate a cattle grid is reached, after which the track becomes a metalled village road for Askham. Continue along this road and descend through the upper level of the village and green to reach once again the cross roads in the village centre and the end of the walk.

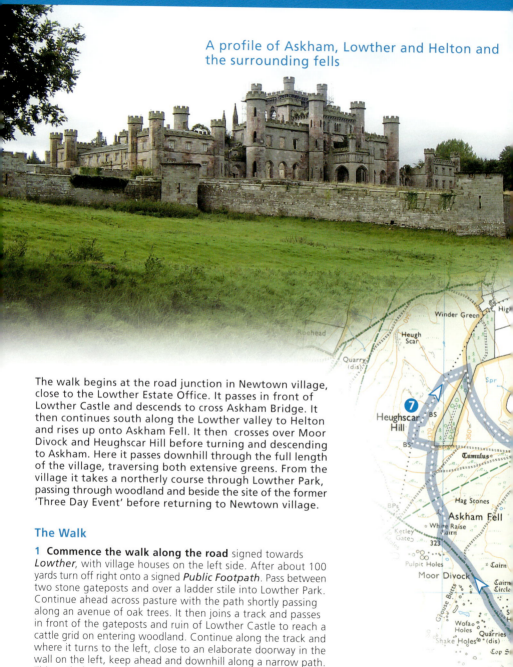

A profile of Askham, Lowther and Helton and the surrounding fells

The walk begins at the road junction in Newtown village, close to the Lowther Estate Office. It passes in front of Lowther Castle and descends to cross Askham Bridge. It then continues south along the Lowther valley to Helton and rises up onto Askham Fell. It then crosses over Moor Divock and Heughscar Hill before turning and descending to Askham. Here it passes downhill through the full length of the village, traversing both extensive greens. From the village it takes a northerly course through Lowther Park, passing through woodland and beside the site of the former 'Three Day Event' before returning to Newtown village.

The Walk

1 Commence the walk along the road signed towards *Lowther*, with village houses on the left side. After about 100 yards turn off right onto a signed *Public Footpath*. Pass between two stone gateposts and over a ladder stile into Lowther Park. Continue ahead across pasture with the path shortly passing along an avenue of oak trees. It then joins a track and passes in front of the gateposts and ruin of Lowther Castle to reach a cattle grid on entering woodland. Continue along the track and where it turns to the left, close to an elaborate doorway in the wall on the left, keep ahead and downhill along a narrow path. This path descends quite steeply, turning to the right at one point, to reach the Newtown to Askham road at Askham Bridge.

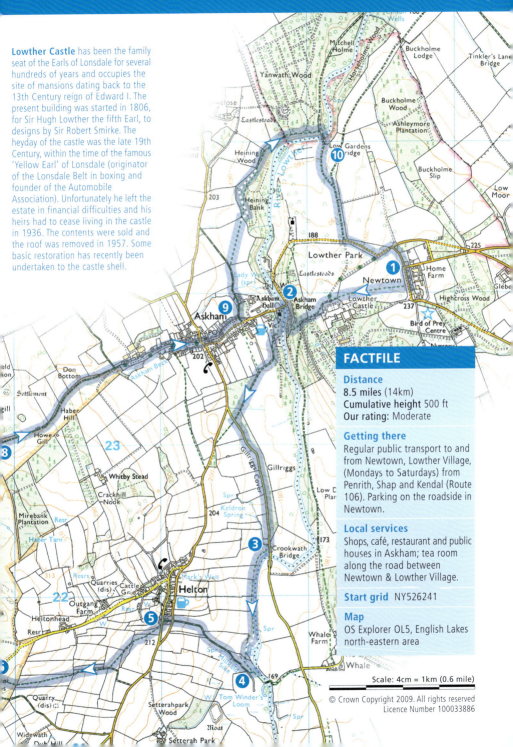

Lowther Castle has been the family seat of the Earls of Lonsdale for several hundreds of years and occupies the site of mansions dating back to the 13th Century reign of Edward I. The present building was started in 1806, for Sir Hugh Lowther the fifth Earl, to designs by Sir Robert Smirke. The heyday of the castle was the late 19th Century, within the time of the famous 'Yellow Earl' of Lonsdale (originator of the Lonsdale Belt in boxing and founder of the Automobile Association). Unfortunately he left the estate in financial difficulties and his heirs had to cease living in the castle in 1936. The contents were sold and the roof was removed in 1957. Some basic restoration has recently been undertaken to the castle shell.

FACTFILE

Distance
8.5 miles (14km)
Cumulative height 500 ft
Our rating: Moderate

Getting there
Regular public transport to and from Newtown, Lowther Village, (Mondays to Saturdays) from Penrith, Shap and Kendal (Route 106). Parking on the roadside in Newtown.

Local services
Shops, café, restaurant and public houses in Askham; tea room along the road between Newtown & Lowther Village.

Start grid NY526241

Map
OS Explorer OL5, English Lakes north-eastern area

Scale: 4cm = 1km (0.6 mile)

St Peter's Church, Askham

2 Turn left, across the bridge, then immediately leave the road to the left, over a stile that leads into the churchyard of St Peter's Church signed *Public Footpath*. Pass to the left side of the church, then veer right and through a gate. Continue uphill along a churchyard path and having passed to the left side of gravestones leave through a gate in the upward boundary wall. Turn left and with woodland to the left side continue to a further gate. Once through turn to the right, as directed and by keeping a wall to the right side pass onto an enclosed track. Follow along the track with woodland to the right. At a left turning in the track, where signs indicate *private* turn off right, over a stile. Pass through the woodland and over a further stile that leads onto the Askham to Whale road (known here as 'Gillriggs Cover'). Turn left, along the road, and go gently downhill for a little over half a mile, towards Crookwath Bridge.

The **River Lowther** is primarily a trout river but is also a spawning area for spring salmon. The flow of the river is regulated to an extent by discharge rates from the Haweswater and Wet Sleddale reservoirs and flows at a fairly consistent rate in all seasons.

3 On approaching Crookwath Bridge turn off the road to the right and through a gate into the corner of a first field. This is opposite where the woodland on the left comes to an end. Once through, turn left, through a second gate and cross a footbridge within the second field. At this point the course of the River Lowther will be close by on the left side. Follow along beside the river with the path traversing a number of fields. Another footbridge is crossed in the second, a stile leads into the third, a footbridge and gate into the fourth, a stile into the fifth and a gate into the sixth. The path passes to the left of a group of large boulders within this sixth field, then veers right, away from the river to a stile in the further right corner in the narrow neck of this field. Once over the stile turn left and follow along the left side of the next field. Where the fence turns away to the left continue ahead and over a gated footbridge across Millfield Sike.

Knipe Scar from Helton

4 From the bridge turn sharp right, away from the river and after a few feet reach a slightly elevated grassy track by a wall corner. Turn right, along this track, cross Millfield Sike once again and rise gently uphill to a gate. From the gate the track is enclosed and for a further third of a mile continues along a somewhat winding course uphill and through a gate (or stile) to reach the Helton 'by-pass' road. Cross over the road and continue along a track, between buildings, signed *Public Bridleway*. Upon reaching a junction with the village road in Helton turn left to shortly reach a signed *Public Footpath* on the right, some steps and a gate.

Footbridge over Millfield Syke

The name **Helton** is derived from 'the settlement on the slope'. It was formerly known as 'Helton-Flecket' (Flecket was a family name) to distinguish it from 'Helton Beacon' which is now known as Hilton.

5 Proceed along the footpath by veering left and uphill from the gate across the first field. Climb over a stile, veer right and continue uphill to reach the upper boundary of the next. Turn left here, through a gate (possibly broken), along the upper right side of a small field enclosure and over a stile. Continue ahead, across the next field to a gate which is set about half way along the opposite boundary wall. Once through turn right, along an enclosed path to a further gate at the end of the enclosure. Continue uphill along the left side of a field that exhibits the remains of old cultivation terraces. At the upper corner climb over a stile (adjoining gate) and make diagonally left across a long upper field to eventually reach a gate and stile at the edge of the Open Access Land of Askham Fell. From this point continue along the grassy path ahead that is broadly on the same alignment as before, to reach the access road from Helton.

Cultivation terraces were often created during the 13th or 14th centuries, and would have been built up to make better use of a sloping area of arable land. The terraces would have made it easier for the mediaeval farmer to make more efficient use of his land. They tended to die out of use following enclosure.

On **Askham Fell** there are numerous archaeological remains, generally from the Bronze Age. These include several stone circles, cairns and tumuli, along with individual standing stones such as the 'Cop Stone'. There is reputed to have been an ancient annual market and fair held on the Fell.

Heughscar Hill is the highest part of Askham Fell, rising to just over 1,200 ft. The course of the 'High Street' Roman Road passes over the western flank of the hill.

Askham village is claimed by many to be the most attractive village in north Cumbria. It is currently associated with the Lowther estate but over the centuries has had associations with Sir Thomas de Hellbeck, the Swynburn family and Edmund de Sandford. The name means 'place of the ash trees.'

6 Cross the road onto a grassy path which is signed *Roe Head 2 miles*. This path passes by a significant stone called 'Cop Stone' and shortly after joins a broad grassy track at a shallow angle. Continue along this track across the section of Askham Fell called Moor Divock. The track passes close to limestone shake holes and also ancient cairns as it takes a straight and fairly level course across the Fell. Where, after about half a mile the track turns noticeably to the left at a high point, turn off right along a grassy fell path that leads uphill towards a woodland corner. Upon reaching the woodland turn left along the broad edge of Heughscar Hill to reach a viewpoint over Ullswater after about 150 yards. From the viewpoint area turn sharp right, off the broad edge and make for the nearby cairn that sits on the shallow summit of Heughscar Hill.

7 Veer right at the summit, then shortly left, onto a grassy path that runs parallel with the woodland edge which is away to the right. When the main path veers left keep ahead on a lesser path, still keeping parallel with the woodland. This path descends very gently towards a shallow valley but is cut by another path that, to the right, leads towards an apparent corner in the woodland. Turn and proceed along this path, which reaches the woodland at a break. Turn sharp right and pass through the woodland break. Once through, continue along a grassy track across the open fell but veer left at any track or path junction. The track gradually turns towards the left and after about a third of a mile comes alongside the plantation wall (on the left) at Riggingleys Top. Once past the plantation it reaches a gate at the edge of Askham Fell.

8 Pass through the gate and continue gently downhill on the grassy, then stone based track. After nearly three quarters of a mile a cattle grid is reached at the upper entrance to Askham village. Once through, proceed along the village street, dropping downhill then passing beside the upper village green to reach the main village crossroads. Cross over and continue along the road between the Queen's Head Inn and Askham Stores. This road drops down the left side of the lower village green. Continue ahead over grass where the road turns sharply right and drop down to a track that then leads left to a gateway with a studded wooden door.

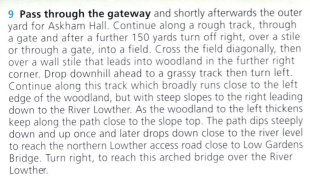

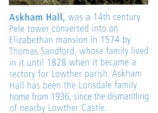

9 **Pass through the gateway** and shortly afterwards the outer yard for Askham Hall. Continue along a rough track, through a gate and after a further 150 yards turn off right, over a stile or through a gate, into a field. Cross the field diagonally, then over a wall stile that leads into woodland in the further right corner. Drop downhill ahead to a grassy track then turn left. Continue along this track which broadly runs close to the left edge of the woodland, but with steep slopes to the right leading down to the River Lowther. As the woodland to the left thickens keep along the path close to the slope top. The path dips steeply down and up once and later drops down close to the river level to reach the northern Lowther access road close to Low Gardens Bridge. Turn right, to reach this arched bridge over the River Lowther.

10 **Keep ahead from the bridge,** through a gate (or stile) around another gate and uphill along the access road. Pass by a junction and over a cattle grid then after a further 300 yards reach the Newtown to Askham road. Turn left and uphill along this road then after crossing a further cattle grid turn right at a road junction onto the road signed *Lowther 1 mile*. Continue uphill to shortly reach the road junction at Newtown village and the end of the walk.

Askham Hall, was a 14th century Pele tower converted into an Elizabethan mansion in 1574 by Thomas Sandford, whose family lived in it until 1828 when it became a rectory for Lowther parish. Askham Hall has been the Lonsdale family home from 1936, since the dismantling of nearby Lowther Castle.

Lowther Horse Trials. This part of the walk route goes through the former Lowther arena and showground, which in early August was the venue for the annual Horse Trials and Country Fair. This was known as 'The Three Day Event'.

Newtown village was built alongside Home Farm to replace the old village which was demolished in the 1680's so as to open up the prospect of Sir John Lowther's house. Newtown village was designed so as to establish a manufacturing facility for linen, although this did not succeed.

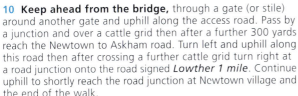

A walk with panoramic views of the Lowther Valley and a gentle ramble beside the River Lowther.

Cross Gate, to the west of Bampton

The walk begins in the centre of Bampton village at the road junction alongside the village shop and Bampton Bridge. A shorter option starts from and finishes at the same point but is less ambitious in the elevations it reaches. For much of the walk good views can be gained up and down the Lowther Valley from field paths that lead across the hillside to and from the open upland at Cockle Hill, above Butterwick. The latter part of the walk crosses the open access land of Green Crook before returning to Bampton along the River Lowther riverside path.

The walk has two circular options:

Option A: A longer moderately strenuous walk that ascends around 500ft from Bampton to the open upland before descending a similar amount to Butterwick. The return from Butterwick is generally flat.

Option B: An easier shorter walk that rises 300ft before cutting across to the returning longer walk and descending to Butterwick. Again the return from Butterwick is generally flat.

Scale: 4cm = 1km (0.6 mile)

The Lowther Valley from Cross Gate

The Walk:

Option A: The Full Walk

1 **From the road junction by the bridge** commence the walk along the village street in the direction signed towards *Penrith*. Pass by an open 'garage' structure on the left then turn left steeply uphill on a minor road. Cross a cattle grid, round various bends and after about a quarter of a mile pass between some buildings. Where the road turns sharply left veer right, steeply uphill, with a wall to the right side and regain the road at a higher elevation. Cross a second cattle grid and a short distance after turn off the road to the right over a stone step stile, onto a signed *Public Footpath*.

2 **Contour diagonally across a field** to locate and climb over a second stone step stile, a little to the right of a gate. Drop downhill in the next field a little way off the wall to the left, towards the right end of a tree copse. After negotiating a further stile and gill rise uphill, veer towards the left across the next field and climb over a ladder stile. Proceed ahead with woodland to the left then, after a further stile, pass through the garden on the left side of the property 'Skews'. Emerge again over a further stile then continue along the right field boundary to a gate and a further such boundary to another gate.

FACTFILE

Distance
Option A: 4 miles (6.5km)
Our rating: Moderate
Option B: 3 miles (5km)
Our rating: Easy

Getting there
Public transport is available from Penrith on Tuesdays and Saturdays only (Bus route 111). Village Hall car park (£1) and roadside parking in and around Bampton.

Local services
Shop/café and inn in Bampton village.

Start grid NY514182

Map
OS Explorer OL5, English Lakes north-eastern area

Path down to Gillhead

Roughill School was founded in 1632 as a result of a bequest of £40 in the will of Edmund Noble. It continued as a centre for the education of local children until about 1950.

3 **Continue ahead** to a stone step stile, then along the left side of a further field. Pass through a gateway and drop downhill ahead to a stile beside a wooded gill. From the stile cross the gill footbridge then rise up steeply to a small gate. From the gate veer left and continue steeply uphill to Low Rough Hill farm to reach a gate on the left side of the first main farm building. From the gate cross a small yard with the former Roughill School building to the left. Pass through a further gate that opens onto the farm access track. Turn immediately sharp right then uphill to another gate. Once through this gate turn sharply left and continue rising uphill with a wall on the immediate left side. Pass through a further gate and at the top of the rise climb over a ladder stile onto the open upland of Cockle Hill.

4 **Once on the upland** locate a gap in the rough grass to the right then turn right and follow a winding path through the grass for about 200 yards, with a wall on the right side. Upon reaching a wall ahead turn right, pass through a gate at the wall corner, then continue along the left edge of a field to a further gate on the left near a tree copse. Once through this gate continue in the same direction as before, downhill along the right side of a field. Pass through a further gate and continue down or alongside the groove of a former track and after passing through another gate reach a 'T' junction with a farm track at Gillhead. Turn right along this track, pass to the right side of Gillhead, cross the bridge over Gill Beck and turn left with the track at a triangular track junction.

5 Continue along a concrete surfaced access road then turn off left, after a cattle grid, over a stone step stile. From the stile veer away from the access road and wall on the right, then once over the hill brow continue downhill towards a stone barn which is the first building the path passes on reaching Butterwick hamlet. Pass through a gate on the left side of the barn then continue into the hamlet along an enclosed track. Cross a footbridge over Gill Beck then turn right along a local road for a few yards to a junction with the Bampton to Penrith road.

6 Turn right, pass over a 'hump backed' bridge then left, off the road, through a field gate onto flat open access common land. Veer left from the gate to cross the common land to locate, then cross a low concrete bridge over Pow Beck. Once over the bridge veer right and make towards the pedestrian suspension bridge over the River Lowther, which will now be visible close to a tree copse. Pass the end of the bridge (don't cross) then continue along the Lowther riverside path. This path follows the river for just over three quarters of a mile. After the initial stile the path later crosses another stile, passes through a small gate then a little distance after veers left to a ladder stile. From the ladder stile it continues to a small gate that leads onto the Shap to Bampton road. Turn right at the road then off again right along a path that parallels the road shortly reaching Bampton and the end of the walk in the village centre.

Option B: The Shorter Circular Walk

Commence the walk in the centre of Bampton village. Follow the direction given in paragraphs 1 and 2 above. Once through a gate described at the end of paragraph 2 turn right through a further gate into a field that is narrow and tapers downhill ahead. Proceed down the right side of this field and pass through a further gate at the far end. Continue ahead across open pasture, with a track joining from the right. Cross a cattle grid then continue ahead across a triangular track junction. From this point follow the route described in paragraphs 5 & 6 above, to eventually return to Bampton.

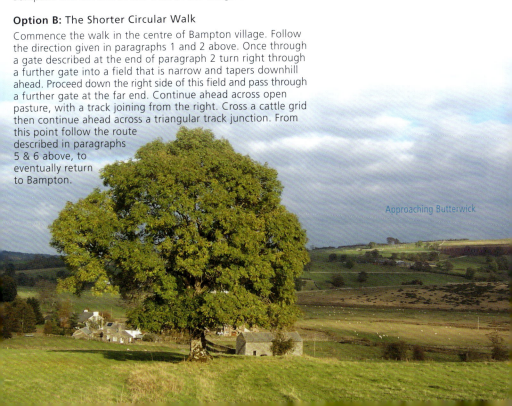

Approaching Butterwick

Walking out from Shap amongst ancient stones and mediaeval monasticism.

Rosgill Bridge

Scale: 4cm = 1km (0.6 mile)

FACTFILE

Distance
5.25 miles (8.5km)
Cumulative height: 600ft
Our rating: Easy

Getting there
Regular public transport from
Penrith or Kendal (Bus route
106). Car park in centre of Shap
village beside A6 road and
Memorial Park.

Local services
Shops, cafés and public houses
in village.

Start grid NY563150

Map
OS Explorer OL5, English Lakes
north-eastern area

The walk begins in the main car park adjoining the Memorial park alongside the A6 in the centre of Shap village. Upon leaving the village it crosses undulating countryside with widescale views of Swindale, Haweswater and the eastern flank of the Lake District. In its central section it progresses up the Lowther Valley from Rosgill, via Shap Abbey, to Keld. The return to Shap allows for a close inspection of the pre-historic 'Goggleby Stone'.

The Walk

1 Turn right, out of the car park, and cross over the A6 at the pedestrian crossing. Pass by the former reading room building then turn off left into a residential side street. Pass two properties on the right, then turn right into a rear access lane. Continue along this lane, behind buildings (various surfaces), to reach the Shap to Bampton road. Turn left and follow along this road as it turns sharp left. After passing a barn turn off right, through a gate, onto a Public Footpath signed to *Rosgill*.

2 Proceed diagonally left across a field to reach a wooden gate in the far corner. Pass through the gate and veer slightly left across the next field and pass through another such gate half way along the further boundary. Continue in the same direction to reach a stone step stile in the far right corner of the next field. When crossing this field look left, to the field across the road, to see a megalith (the Thunder Stone). Climb over the stile onto the road and turn right. Shortly reach another such stile on the left, signed as a *Public Footpath*.

3 Climb over this stile and walk uphill across the left diagonal of a field, through disturbed ground to the left of a lime kiln and climb over a stile in the field corner. Follow along the left edge of the next field and shortly after the first field corner reach a stone step stile in the boundary wall. Turn right after climbing over this stile to reach a further such stile in the far left corner of the next field. From this section of the walk views can be gained of the High Street fells and the Haweswater valley. After climbing over this stile the route veers slightly left and descends across four fields crossing stone step stiles at the edge of each (one also having a gate) before a small wooden gate is reached at the edge of the fourth. Once through this gate continue downhill across the right diagonal of another field to reach a further gate at the lower corner. Pass through the gate and bear right to the next field corner. Climb over the stone step stile near this corner, and follow the wall on your left to a second such stile then a wooden kissing gate. Traverse a garden and drop down from a final stone step stile between cottages to reach the Rosgill village street.

Public footpath through a 'private' garden in Rosgill

Riverside pasture at Rosgill

4 **Turn left** and walk 500 yards down the village street to reach Rosgill Bridge across the River Lowther. Cross over the bridge and turn left at the road corner, through a gate onto a path signed *Public Footpath: Coast to Coast*. Proceed along a grassy track on the right edge of a riverside pasture and pass through a small wooden gate on the right. Once through the gate veer off the track to the left, alongside a wall. Climb over a stone step stile and continue, keeping the wall, then a fence, to the left side to reach a former packhorse bridge (Parish Crag Bridge) across Tailbert Gill.

5 **Once across the bridge veer left** up a steep bank, then continue ahead up a steeply sloping field and climb over a stone step stile that leads into a smaller walled enclosure. Cross the enclosure lengthways and pass through a gate onto a metalled access road. Continue ahead along the road then shortly turn off left over a wooden stile and cross a field to a stone step stile. Once over this stile veer to the right across the contour of the hillside. Cross a grassy track and pass under an electricity line. Contour further, with a wall line to the right side. Close in on the wall, as it turns around to the left and descends. Cross some small gills then continue to a ladder stile at the top of a slight rise. Once over the stile turn right and contour again, with the River Lowther downhill to the left and Shap Abbey visible ahead. Where the river cuts in and the steep river bank is met ahead turn to the right and contour around to reach a further ladder stile. Once over the stile drop steeply down left to the access path to Shap Abbey.

Shap Abbey was Westmorland's only abbey. It was constructed by the Premonstratensian Order of canons in the 12th Century and dedicated to St Mary Magdalene. The ruins are dominated by the 15th Century west tower which was constructed by Richard Redman, the abbot at the time.

6 **Turn right, along the path** for a visit to the Shap Abbey ruins, then return to this point and continue through the gate. Cross over the River Lowther by Abbey Bridge, pass by a dwelling then proceed ahead across a road junction and up the embankment ahead. At the top of the embankment turn right to a stone step stile and gate. Continue along the right side of the next field to reach another such stile and gate. In the next follow the left-hand field wall to reach a stone step stile set in this wall. Climb over the stile and continue in the same direction as before with the wall now on the right side. When this wall turns sharp right, bear slightly right towards the wall corner in front of you. From this corner veer right, cross a section of field and pass to the right of a further wall corner. Keep the field boundary to the left and cross a field indentation to reach a wooden ladder stile that leads into a play area beside a tennis court at Keld. Once over the stile, cross the play area and pass beside a dwelling to the village street.

7 **Turn left, up the street** and shortly pass 15th Century Keld Chapel on the right side. Pass the road junction to Thornship Township and shortly after turn off the road to the right, over a stone step stile onto a path signed as a *Public Footpath* to *Shap*. Continue in the same direction as before and follow the field boundary with the road to the left. Climb over a stone step stile in the upper field corner and at the path junction (50 yards further on) continue in the same general direction. Cross a broken down wall into the next field and continue to a further stone step stile that leads into a green lane. Cross the lane and another such stile then continue along the left edge of the next field. This field contains the Goggleby stone, a megalith which is part of a stone circle about a mile in diameter. Once past the stone climb over another stone step stile, pass a plantation and over yet another such stile. Continue uphill in a narrow field, then descend again to a gate. Pass between dwellings to another gate which opens onto the rear access lane used at the beginning of the walk. Turn right, along this lane, and retrace your steps the short distance back, across the A6 road to the car park and the end of the walk.

Keld Chapel, which is owned by the National Trust, can be visited. The key can be obtained from the cottage opposite. The chapel is thought to have been constructed as a Chantry chapel.

A hillside walk to Haweswater, Thornthwaite Force and the upper Lowther Valley

FACTFILE

Distance
8.5 miles (13.75km)
Our rating: Moderate

Getting there
Public transport is available from Penrith on Tuesdays and Saturdays only (Bus route 111). Village Hall car park (£1) and roadside parking in and around Bampton.

Local services
Shop/café and public house in Bampton village.

Start grid NY514182

Map
OS Explorer OL5, English Lakes north-eastern area

The walk begins in the centre of Bampton village at the road junction alongside the village shop and Bampton Bridge. The walk rises up to the west of the village onto the hillsides of Bampton Common before descending to the waterfalls of Measand Beck and the path beside Haweswater Reservoir. It returns to Bampton through Burnbanks, past Thornthwaite Force and Rosgill Bridge then by field paths alongside the River Lowther.

Haweswater reservoir

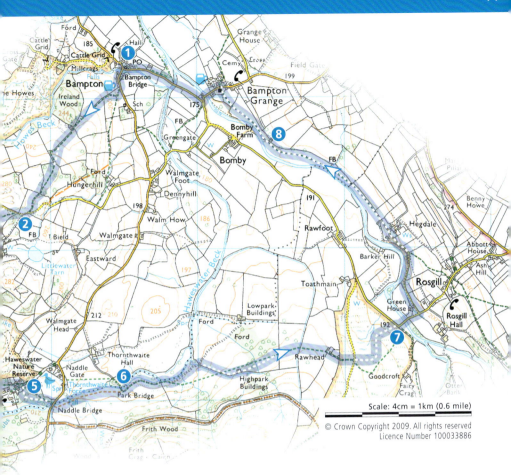

Scale: 4cm = 1km (0.6 mile)

The Walk

1 From the road junction cross over Bampton Bridge and
along the road signed to *Haweswater*. Pass by Mardale Inn,
St. Patrick's Well and after the end of village buildings turn off
the road to the right, onto a track signed as a *Public Footpath*.
Pass through some gates and continue uphill along a grassy
track which soon turns sharply to the right, then later to the
left. With the field boundary then on the right side cross the
line of an old wall and as the hillside flattens a little continue
to a gate (adjoining stile), close to a barn. From the gate pass
to the side of a tree clump then proceed ahead on the right
side of the field. Veer uphill to the left after traversing about
half of the field to reach a ladder stile at the upper field boundary.
From the stile veer left, through a grazed enclosure of mature
trees, then gradually approach a wall boundary on the right
side. Once alongside the wall pass through a gate at the far
corner of the enclosure. Continue along a stone track to reach
a gate that leads onto a local access road.

Bampton village, the 'settlement by
the tree', was formerly one of three
manors, each containing Bampton as
part of their titles. Whilst the village
might appear to have been a quiet
backwater in the 19th century it
supported tradespeople such as
tailors, shoemakers, joiners, grocers,
butchers, clog makers, master
blacksmiths and a miller.

Round Table from Pinnacle Howe

2 Turn right, along this road and pass by an access on the left leading to Littlewater. After a further few yards turn left off the road, over a stile, onto a path signed *Public Footpath*. Skirt around to the right side of the rocky hillock ahead in this field and once around locate, then make for a ladder stile over the further boundary wall.

Drybarrows

From this stile veer slightly to the left to reach a second ladder stile, then slightly to the right across a field corner to a third such stile. The path then crosses diagonally left and uphill across the next field (with a gill mid field) to a fourth ladder stile. From this stile turn to the left and proceed uphill then ahead over a hill brow. Once over continue ahead, with a wall to the right, to reach a gate in the field corner. Once through, climb up steeply and, keeping a wall to the right, pass by the property known as Drybarrows. Once past, veer right to gain a grassy track which exits out of Drybarrows with a tree plantation now to the right side.

3 Proceed ahead on the grassy track across boggy ground then steeply uphill on a furrowed track to the saddle between two small hills, the left one of which is called Pinnacle Howe. Once across the saddle veer slightly round to the right and continue along the track, descending a little to the ford of Intack Sike. Cross the Sike and continue ahead and uphill along a clear grassy track between bracken.

Avoid paths that turn off and uphill to the right side and as the path begins to contour make towards a gap ahead between the hills to the left and the main hill to the right. Upon reaching the gap the path passes beside a small tarn and some cairns. From the gap continue downhill and ahead along the mainly grassy path which crosses the slope of the hillside to the right. The path makes towards the valley ahead of Measand Beck, with Haweswater coming into view to the left. Keep ahead and look out for the footbridge in the valley, towards which the path will lead. The distance between the gap and the footbridge is about three quarters of a mile. Gradually descend, crossing some boggy sections, to reach the Measand Beck footbridge.

4 Cross over the footbridge then turn to the left and follow the path downhill alongside the Beck, passing waterfalls, with a little rock scrambling to reach the path along the north side of Haweswater Reservoir. It is quite possible to avoid any rock scrambling by turning away from the Beck and descending by a grassy path a little distance from the Beck. Turn left, along the path, cross Measand Beck by a further footbridge then proceed for about one and a quarter miles alongside the reservoir.

Pass by the reservoir dam and woodland to eventually reach a gate in the right fence, where the track enters the woodland near Burnbanks. Pass through this gate and continue downhill on the track as it zig zags through the woodland, through a further gate, then past a number of dwellings to reach a junction of tracks by the small Burnbanks car park.

Haweswater reservoir is now one of the largest of the 'lakes'. It is four miles long and half a mile wide with a maximum depth of 200 feet. In 1929 a bill was passed by Parliament authorising the use of Haweswater as a reservoir for Manchester and the conurbations of north west England. A concrete dam, 1550 feet wide and 120 feet high was built, which raised the former lake level by 95 feet. To construct the reservoir the farms and houses of the villages of Mardale Green and Measand were demolished along with Mardale church, stone from which was used in the dam construction. The reservoir is home to the rare schelly fish.

Bridge over Measand Beck

Burnbanks village was built to accommodate the families of the workforce who built Haweswater Dam for Manchester Corporation. Sixty-six bungalows were built, together with a mission room, recreation hall and huts for single workmen. Today about a third of the bungalows remain and these have recently been refurbished and updated.

Thornthwaite means the clearing by the thorn trees (probably hawthorn). The waterfall that forms Thornthwaite Force is over 20ft in height and in times of flood on Haweswater Beck provides quite a spectacle of water power.

Park Bridge

5 Cross over the junction and pass through a gate at the back of the car park into woodland on a Public Footpath signed for *Naddle Bridge*. Follow this path as it winds through the woodland and emerges after about a quarter of a mile over a step stile on to the road at Naddle Bridge. Cross straight over the road and descend a ladder stile the other side, cross over the Haweswater Beck on the old bridge (no parapets), then proceed across a footbridge and meadow land parallel with the river to a ladder stile close to Thornthwaite Force. From this stile continue alongside the river on a path strewn with tree roots, crossing a number of small plank bridges to reach the end of Park Bridge, which crosses the Beck.

6 Don't cross the bridge but continue along a grassy and rough beckside track to a wooden stile close to the Beck. From the stile continue along the track, eventually following it steeply uphill to a gate and wooden stile. Turn right, from the stile and continue up a steep path with a fence on the immediate right side. Pass by farm buildings then, as the land flattens out, veer away from the fence, with the path, and continue across meadow land to a further stile. Cross over the next field to another such stile then veer to the right, across the brow of the following field and downhill to a gate and stile alongside the residential property known as Rawhead. Continue along the concrete tracked drive of Rawhead, cross a cattle grid and shortly reach the metalled road to Swindale. Cross over this road and follow the footpath opposite, downhill at first and over some boggy land. Veer left across scrub land then descend right to a wall and ladder stile near Rosgill Bridge.

7 From the stile proceed ahead along the road across Rosgill Bridge. Pass Green House on the left then turn left onto a narrow metalled road with a sign pointing to *Hegdale*. Follow this road for nearly half a mile, with the River Lowther on the left side, eventually reaching a point where the road turns sharply right, into Hegdale Farm. At this point continue straight ahead along an enclosed track to reach a stile (and gate) located to the immediate right side of a barn. Once over, proceed ahead, along the right side of a riverside pasture. Pass through a gate at the further end then continue along the centre of the next pasture to reach a footbridge, gate and stile. From here continue along the length of a third section of pasture, this time curving slightly with trees on the right to reach a stone stile in the far right corner. Climb over this stile, cross a green lane and climb over a further wall stile.

8 Continue along the length of another riverside field to a gate located about mid length along the far boundary. Proceed then along the left side of the next field to a kissing gate in the boundary of St Patrick's Churchyard at Bampton Grange. From the gate pass through the churchyard to the right of the church to reach a gate that leads out onto the main street of the village opposite the Crown and Mitre Public House. Turn left in the village and follow the road across the bridge over the River Lowther. Turn sharp right at a road junction along the road signed to *Helton, Askham & Penrith*. Just after the road crosses the bridge over Haweswater Beck, go through the second of two small gates on the right and follow a path parallel to the road and then a pavement to reach the road junction in the centre of Bampton and the end point of the walk.

Rosgill means 'the ravine of the horses'. For many centuries the manor, which is in Shap parish, was held by a succession of families, including a John de Rosgill. It eventually became part of the Lowther estate. The bridge has been controversial in the past due to its narrowness and problems with animals falling to their deaths over the parapets.

St Patrick's church was built in 1726 (restored in 1885) on a site which has been used for worship from the 12th century when it was connected to the Premonstratensian monks at Shap Abbey. The church lych gate constructed in 1929 from Haweswater Estate oak, was a gift from Manchester Corporation.

Rosgill Bridge and the village beyond

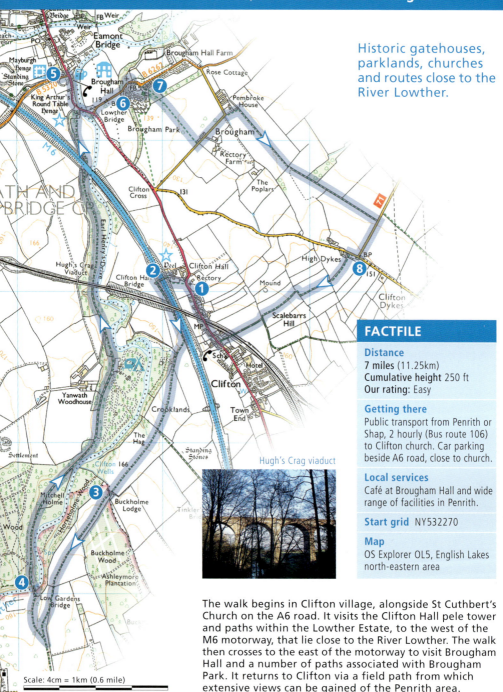

Historic gatehouses, parklands, churches and routes close to the River Lowther.

Hugh's Crag viaduct

FACTFILE

Distance
7 miles (11.25km)
Cumulative height 250 ft
Our rating: Easy

Getting there
Public transport from Penrith or Shap, 2 hourly (Bus route 106) to Clifton church. Car parking beside A6 road, close to church.

Local services
Café at Brougham Hall and wide range of facilities in Penrith.

Start grid NY532270

Map
OS Explorer OL5, English Lakes north-eastern area

The walk begins in Clifton village, alongside St Cuthbert's Church on the A6 road. It visits the Clifton Hall pele tower and paths within the Lowther Estate, to the west of the M6 motorway, that lie close to the River Lowther. The walk then crosses to the east of the motorway to visit Brougham Hall and a number of paths associated with Brougham Park. It returns to Clifton via a field path from which extensive views can be gained of the Penrith area.

The walk

1 From the car parking area cross over the A6 road to a wall stile immediately opposite St Cuthbert's Church. Climb over the stile onto a public footpath that leads towards Clifton Hall: a pele tower which is under the custodianship of English Heritage. Continue ahead along the right side of a paddock and climb over a stile in the far corner. Pass along an enclosed path and through a kissing gate onto a concrete farm road. The walk then turns left onto the road, but before proceeding take the opportunity to visit Clifton Hall, the pele tower across the road to the right.

Clifton Hall is a small 16th Century pele tower which stands on its own beside a farmyard. The tower (33 ft by 26 ft) has three storeys, the ground floor being divided into a number of rooms. The windows are larger than in earlier peles and there is a newel stair in the south-west corner leading to the upper rooms and roof. Excavations have uncovered the remains of a Mediaeval hall and cross-wing.

Lowther Castle has been the family seat of the Earls of Lonsdale from time immemorial, and occupies the site of mansions dating back to the 13th Century reign of Edward I. The present building was started in 1806, for Sir Hugh Lowther the fifth Earl, to designs by Sir Robert Smirke. Lowther Castle was his first job when he was 25 and was commissioned to be a design of elegance and strength. The heyday of the castle was during the late 19th Century, within the time of the famous "Yellow Earl" of Lonsdale (originator of the Lonsdale Belt in boxing and founder of the Automobile Association). Unfortunately he left the estate in financial difficulties and his heirs had to cease living in the castle in 1936. The contents were sold and the roof was removed in 1957. Some restoration has recently been undertaken to the castle shell.

2 After visiting the tower proceed along the farm road and cross the bridge over the M6 motorway. Once over, turn left through a gate and continue along a track with the motorway on the immediate left side. Pass under the West Coast main line railway, through a gate and upon nearing another gate veer off right with the track, away from the motorway. Pass through a further gate close to the corner of a woodland and continue along the now grassy track, across pasture, to reach a stile. Continue ahead from the stile, still on a grassy track and after a further third of a mile reach Lowther Estate's Buckholme Lodge. This marks the edge of the formal Lowther Park.

King Arthur's Round Table is an ancient henge which lies close to the Eamont and Lowther rivers. It dates from the late Neolithic and Bronze Ages, more than 3,000 years ago. The henge contains an earth bank and circular ditch a little over 160 ft in diameter. Parts of the henge have been lost through the A6 and B5320 roads truncating the structure. In 1820 it was further desecrated by a local pub landlord who trucked in landfill to raise the centre and proceeded to use it for a tea garden. The henge has nothing to do with the legendary King Arthur it is named after. It was supposedly named in the 14th century when the Clifford family moved into nearby Brougham Castle. They claimed Welsh royal ancestry, which at the time was thought in turn to be descended from the legendary King Arthur.

Clifton Moor was the location of the last battle to be fought on English soil on 18th & 19th December 1745. This was a skirmish known as the Battle of Clifton during the retreat of Bonnie Prince Charlie in the 1745 Rebellion. A gravestone in the church yard at Clifton commemorates the troopers who were killed in the battle whereas the Scots who fell are said to share a mass grave under a nearby large tree at the south of the village, known as the 'Rebel Tree'.

3 Pass through the gate beside the Lodge and continue ahead along a stony track. The track passes through a gate at a tree belt then rises up gently across pasture. It crosses a cattle grid and after two thirds of a mile from the Lodge descends to a junction with a metalled estate road. Ahead at this point will be glimpses of Lowther Castle. Upon reaching this junction turn sharply to the right and continue along the metalled estate road as it descends, with the former Lowther showground to the left.

The road passes through a gate (which walkers can skirt around), and reaches a stile and gate at Low Gardens Bridge over the River Lowther. This part of the walk route goes through the former Lowther arena and showground, which in early August was the venue for the annual Horse Trials and Country Fair. This was known as 'The Three Day Event'.

4 Cross over the bridge and continue ahead through the Lowther woodlands along a major estate road. After about two thirds of a mile pass through a gate into the Lowther Caravan Park. The route passes between caravans and chalets to reach the park's entrance barrier. Once past the barrier continue along the metalled access road (Earl Henry's Drive) for a further three quarters of a mile, passing under Hugh's Crag Viaduct on the West Coast main line and the M6 motorway to reach the A6 road through the exit gates to Lowther Park. At this point continue ahead along the left pavement of the A6 to reach a junction with the B5320 road by a war memorial. Turn left here and after a further few yards turn off left, through a gate, to visit the pre-historic henge known as 'King Arthur's Round Table'.

Boundary wall and gateway,
Brougham Hall

5 Leave the henge and turn right, back to the road junction
with the A6. Turn right again, but cross the road onto the
opposite footpath. Follow this path and cross over Lowther
Bridge on that road. Immediately after the bridge turn off left
onto the B6262 road and follow this past meadows. Continue
uphill between retaining walls and under an archway that joins
Brougham (*pronounced 'broom'*) Hall to St Wilfrid's Church. As
the left wall comes to an end turn off the road to the left then
turn left again into the churchyard. Pass beside the church then
turn left, once again, through gates to cross the bridge into the
outer grounds of Brougham Hall.

6 Pass around the outer walls of the hall where various
notices describe the history of the ruins. The area also contains
a plaque, unveiled in 2003, to the Clifton Moor battle. At the
further end of the grassy route reach the vehicular access into
the inner area of Brougham Hall. Here the opportunity can be
taken to turn left and visit businesses and the cafe before
returning back to this spot. Continue then ahead, with the walls
to Brougham Hall on the left and housing to the right, along
Brougham Hall Gardens. Turn around to the left with the road,
then right at the next road junction onto the right pavement of
a straight residential street with the majority of dwellings on
the left side. Pass by a public footpath sign that leads across
the corner of a garden then, a few yards past the end of the
garden wall, locate a path (probably unsigned) that leads across
rough grass into a thicket. *[Note: this is not immediately alongside
the wall]*

Brougham Hall is a 13th century
fortified manor house, founded by
Gilbert de Broham. In 1307, Ricardus
de Brun of Dummaloch founded the
stone hall when he was granted a
licence to crenellate. In the 16th
century there was a complex range of
buildings, which included a manor
house, a byre and a gate, to which a
17th century pele tower was added.
Later in the 17th century, Lady Anne
Clifford restored the hall. The site was
largely rebuilt in the 19th century,
after it was repossessed and extended
by Lord Brougham, Lord Chancellor
from 1830 to 1834. The historic home
of the Brougham family fell into ruins
in the 1930's but more recently a
gradual programme of restoration has
been underway. A range of craft
workshops, a tea room and a gift shop
have been established within the
impressive outer walls.

Leafy lane leading away from
Brougham towards High Dykes

7 **Proceed along the path** and pass through the thicket on a winding route to reach a stile on the far side. Once over the stile veer slightly right and make across a field to a gate immediately to the right side of a dwelling. Pass through this gate, cross a small enclosure and pass through a further gate that leads onto a country road. Turn left, along this road, to reach a sharp left bend on the road. At this point turn off right, over a stile (or through a gate), onto a Public Footpath signed to *Moor Lane*. Proceed along this path in the same direction as before, up the short left side of a field. At the corner turn sharp right and follow the long left side for about a third of a mile to reach three gates set at the far end. Pass through the middle one of the gates onto a shrub and tree lined green lane. Continue along the lane in a straight line for nearly half a mile to eventually reach a gate that leads onto a further country road. Turn right, along the road to reach a junction with the Eamont Bridge to Cliburn road.

8 **Turn right at the junction** signed to *Penrith* then after a short distance turn off left over a stone step stile onto a signed *Public Footpath*. *[Note: This stile is quite narrow and may prove difficult for some people to squeeze through. If this is the case a gate is located a few yards back which leads into the same enclosure. This might be a suitable alternative but if used the path should be re-gained again behind the stile.]* Proceed ahead between buildings and climb over a stile into a field. Continue along the right side of the field and pass through a gate at the far corner. Continue ahead but this time along the left side of the next field, and then turn right at the far end to reach a stile in the left boundary. Climb over the stile and once again proceed ahead, up the left side of a rising field then at the far end veer left to a further stile. Climb over the stile and turn right, along an unmade track. Cross over the West Coast main line and after passing between dwellings reach the A6 road at Clifton. Turn right, along the right pavement of the A6, cross over the railway once again then return to the parking area close to St Cuthbert's Church and the end of the walk.

St Cuthbert's Church is built on a site which has probably contained a church for over a thousand years. Tradition has it that this was one of the resting places of St Cuthbert's remains. In the 9th Century the monks took the body of the saint, who died in 687AD, and fled the Viking raids, carrying the body with them. It now rests in Durham Cathedral. The Church has a Norman doorway, and the oldest part of the building is the 12th Century nave. The church was given to Clifton by Lord Brougham of Brougham Hall. Ten of the English Dragoons who were killed by Jacobite forces in the 1745 Battle of Clifton were buried in the churchyard. There is a stone near the Church gate to commemorate the incident.

St Cuthbert's Church, Clifton

Walking
in the
Eden Valley

3

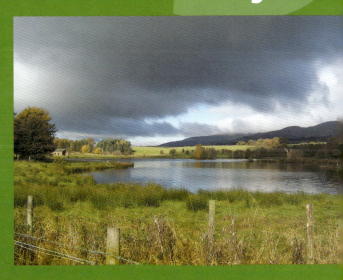

r

ramblers
at the heart of walking

FACTFILE

Distance
6.5 miles (10.5km)
Cumulative height: 500ft
Our rating: Moderate

Getting there
Roadside parking is available
close to Armathwaite Bridge.
Regular train services serve
Armathwaite on the Settle-
Carlisle Railway, from Carlisle,
Appleby and other stations.
Suitable bus services from
Langwathby on a Friday (131)
and Penrith on a Saturday (133)

Local services
Fox & Pheasant Inn and Dukes
Head Inn at Armathwaite; New
Crown Inn at Ainstable.

Start grid NY507460

Map
OS Explorer OL5, English Lakes
north-eastern area

Riverside paths, forest walks and open farmland paths in the Eden Valley

The walk begins at Armathwaite Bridge that crosses the
River Eden just to the east of the village centre. From steps
at the end of the bridge it passes beneath and then follows
close to the bank of the River before rising up through
Coombs Wood. On leaving the woodland it passes through
hamlets at Longdales, Bascodyke and Rowfoot and into
Ainstable village. The return to Armathwaite crosses
farmland with good Eden valley views. It then drops down
to follow alongside the River Eden back to Armathwaite
Bridge.

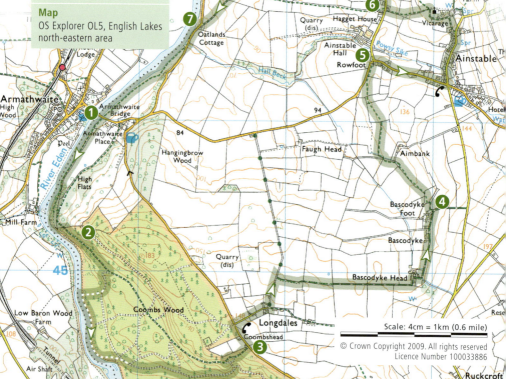

Scale: 4cm = 1km (0.6 mile)

The Walk

1 Commence the walk on Armathwaite Bridge. Armathwaite Bridge provides a good viewpoint of the River Eden, which has flowed through a deeply incised valley from the south. The river flows over flat sandstone slabs as it passes Armathwaite Castle. Walk off the bridge, away from the village and turn off left at a sign that indicates *Public Footpath (under bridge)*. Cross an iron 'step over', descend some stone steps and pass through a small wooden gate. Turn left towards the River Eden by a belt of riverside trees and drop down a little to pass beneath an arch of the bridge, onto a wooded riverside path. Armathwaite Castle can be viewed across the river from this path. Proceed along the path amongst mature trees for a distance of about half a mile to a path junction where some rapids can be seen in the river on the right.

[Note: You may drop down the path to the right here, to take a closer look at the rapids and riverside environment. Return then back to the path junction].

Armathwaite Place. The building started life as a four storey Pele tower, to ward off the border raiders. The property was owned by the Skelton family for several centuries. The family included a number of parliamentarians over the years. One, John Skelton, was Poet Laureate to Henry VIII.

Armathwaite Bridge

Riverside path through Coombs Wood

The **Benchmark sculpture**, 'Vista' by Graeme Mitcheson, is designed on the theme of walking and being at one with nature. The Benchmark can serve as a seat at a fine viewpoint along the river Eden. The sculpture acts as a sun dial with the shadow cast by one of the strewn trouser legs.

Cross the junction and continue along the rising path ahead, above the river, to a point where two fence ends join and abut the path. Turn left here and proceed uphill, across tree roots, until the path comes alongside a wooden stile in the fence to the left. Turn right, away from the stile and proceed along a forest track shortly reaching the Eden Benchmark stone sculpture 'Vista'.

2 View the sculpture and also the river vista below then continue along the forest track within Coombs Wood for about 300 yards. At a junction of tracks turn sharply to the right and descend quite steeply through woodland along another forest track, in the direction of the River Eden. After about 200 yards, when nearing the foot of the descent, turn right, off the track onto an earth based path. Drop steeply down for a short distance then cross a flat section of valley bottom to reach a hut beside the river Eden. Turn left and continue along a riverside path. After about a quarter of a mile the path rises up to the left, away from the river and leads back to the wider forest track. Upon reaching the track turn right and follow it gently, then more steeply uphill for nearly half a mile. At the top of the rise commanding views will be obtained of the river valley towards the south. As the track flattens out turn off to the left and continue on a steep section of path that winds uphill through trees to reach a junction with the main Coombs Wood track. Turn right, still uphill, along this track and shortly come to the forest access gateway and small car park at Coombshead on the Armathwaite to Kirkoswald road.

Coombshead

3 Turn left along the road for a short distance to a road junction signed to Longdales. Turn right along the cul de sac road into Longdales hamlet and where the public road ends turn left onto a track signed *To Bridleway*. Rise up gently along this route to the top of the incline then turn off right, over a stile (or through a gate), onto a bridleway signed *Bascodyke*. Continue along this bridleway for about half a mile, heading in a relatively straight course to the east. Pass through two gates and eventually drop downhill to reach a third at the entrance to Bascodyke Head farmstead. Once through, turn sharp left between some farm buildings, then right, through another gate, avoiding the farm house area. Turn left again, at the farmstead boundary onto the main farm access road. Follow this through gates and past the property Bascodyke, to the point where it turns sharply right beside the entrance to Bascodyke Foot farmstead.

River Eden from Coombs Wood

Bascodyke

4 At this point turn sharp left into the farmstead entrance and across right to a gate. Pass through, then gently downhill through a second, then a third gate in quick succession. Once through the third veer to the left, across a field corner, to a fourth in the lower left corner. Continue then along the left side of a field to reach a stile that leads into an enclosed path. Proceed then along the path as it passes the property 'Aimbank', through a gate and ends beside a ford. Turn right, through the ford, then make up the left side of a field to reach a stile at the upper left corner. Once over, veer left across the corner of the next field to reach a second stile, along the short edge of the next to a third stile and ahead across the next to reach a fourth stile. At this point the Armathwaite to Ainstable road will be close by on the left side and Rowfoot Chapel will be visible ahead. Continue along the left side of the next field and out onto the road through a gate beside the chapel.

5 Turn right, along the road then continue from the nearby junction along the route signed to *Ainstable* and *Kirkoswald*. At the road junction in Ainstable village centre turn sharp left and after passing between dwellings turn off left onto the church access road which is signed: *Public Footpath: Towngate, Ainstable Church*. Follow along the road uphill then left and pass in front of the church, to a gate at the access road end. Pass through the gate, turn right and along the field edge and through a second gate. Once through turn left and along the left edges of three smallish fields, each separated by a stile and dropping downhill. The stile at the corner of the third field leads onto a short length of enclosed path. Continue along this path and through a gate beside a dwelling to reach the Rowfoot to Brampton road.

Ainstable was a Viking settlement and the name describes a 'bracken covered hill' but is a corruption of 'On-Steep-Hill'. The church of St Michael & All Angels dates from 1872, but the site has had a church for more than 900 years. The physician John Leake was born in Ainstable in 1729. He was known as the 'Man-Midwife' and founded the Westminster Lying-in Hospital. He died in 1792 and is buried in Westminster Abbey.

6 Turn right, along the road for about 250 yards. Turn off left onto a public footpath signed to *Armathwaite* and *Oatlands Cottage* and pass through a gate into the yard of Towngate farmstead. Leave the yard through a gate ahead, then proceed along the right side of a field to a further gate. Once through, veer slightly to the right, and cross the next field to another gate. Cross the next field to a stile, then continue along the right edge of the following to a gate. In the next field follow along the right side, then at the right corner turn left, onto a grassy path and continue, still within the field, to the next corner. Pass through a gate onto an enclosed path, signed to *Oatlands Cottage*, then continue along this path, dropping gradually downhill, to reach the Armathwaite to Castle Carrock road.

7 Turn left, along the road and drop down to the bridge over Hall Beck. Once over, turn off right and over a stile, onto a Public Footpath signed to *Armathwaite*. From the stile the path route is close to the Eden river bank. Cross two footbridges then pass through a fence gap. Regain the river bank and continue for about a quarter of a mile to reach Armathwaite Bridge once again. Pass through the gate, up the steps and over the iron 'step over' onto the road. Turn right onto Armathwaite Bridge and the end of the walk.

A fellside walk in the North Pennines with the prospect of panoramic views of the Eden Valley, the Lake District and the Scottish Borders.

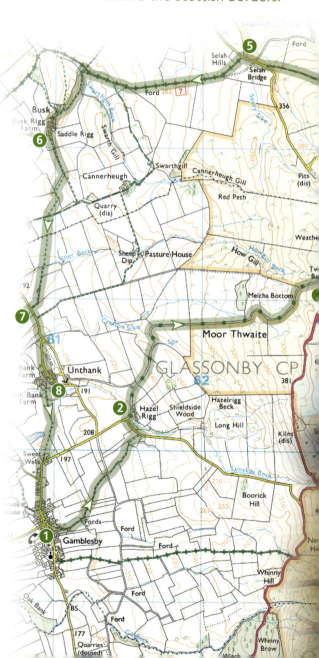

Gamblesby is a village of Norse origin whose name means 'Farmstead' or 'village of a man called Gamall'. The village developed in a protective form against Scottish raiders with farm buildings within the village perimeter and a large green which could be utilised to graze stock. In 1772 John Wesley first preached in Gamblesby and the village, whose first chapel was built in 1784, became the cradle of Methodism in the area of the present county of Cumbria.

Scale: 4cm = 1km (0.6 mile)

Shake
Holes

549

Shake
Holes

7

Ricter Gill

Spr

7

522

Shake Holes

575

Level
(dis)

Hartside
Cross

BS

Level
(dis)

Quarries
(dis)
Green Fell

Hartside Top
(Cafe)

4

Gamblesby Fell

Greenfell
Raise

BS

Quarries
(dis)

BS

Sheepfold

Twotop Hill

Quarry
(dis)

Cairn

Cairn

Shake Holes

FACTFILE

Distance
8 miles (12.7km)
Cumulative height: 1550 ft
Our rating: Strenuous

Getting there
Public transport to and from
Gamblesby is sporadic. The
Fellrunner bus serves the village
from Langwathby on a Thursday
(Route 137) and Friday (Route
131), with a return journey
possible by prior booked
arrangement only. On-road
parking is available within the
village, beside the green.

Local services
Café at Hartside, along the route
of the walk; café and inns in
Melmerby and Langwathby

Start grid NY609395

Map
OS Explorer OL31, North
Pennines, Teesdale & Weardale

Gamblesby, Hartside & Busk

The walk begins in the centre of Gamblesby, close to the village stocks. It then uses old fellside tracks and paths that lead up the slopes of Gamblesby Fell to the Hartside Café, the highest café in England. The walk descends by another old fellside route via Selah Bridge to the hamlet of Busk. It then returns to Gamblesby by field paths, passing through the hamlet of Unthank.

Track to Hartside near Hazel Rigg

The Walk

This **Public Byway** formed part of the pre McAdam route between Penrith and Alston, over Hartside. (The Hartside road which now forms the A686 was constructed under the direction of John McAdam circa 1823). The route would have been used by John Wesley when travelling on horseback from the North East, to preach in Gamblesby and beyond. The track winds somewhat and whilst there is a little undulation there are some steep rising sections. In common with several Pennine tracks it includes a straight section (350yds).

1 Commence the walk from the main crossroads in the village centre, along the road signed as a *Public Footpath* to *Hazel Rigg* (opposite the road signed to Little Salkeld). With a roadside stream to the left pass between dwellings and where the metalled road ends continue out of the village along an enclosed unmade track. This proceeds gently uphill and shortly crosses a slab footbridge to one side at a ford. After about a third of a mile a junction of tracks is reached. Pass across the junction onto a grassy path and shortly climb over a stile into a field. Continue along the right side of the field, over a stone stile, then along the left side of a second field to drop steeply down to a gate. Pass through the gate and turn left along the local road to a corner at Hazel Rigg where a stone track signed as a *Public Byway* to *Twotop Bridge* turns off to the right.

2 Proceed along this track, which firstly passes by Hazel Rigg farmstead. It then begins to rise steadily uphill as an enclosed track onto the lower slopes of Gamblesby Fell. After about half a mile of climbing the track reaches the A686, Penrith to Alston road.

3 Cross diagonally left over the road and onto the metalled access road to the Hartside telecommunications tower. *[Note: Great care is needed in crossing the road at this point due to poor visibility and fast moving traffic, often motorcycles]* Pass over a cattle grid and continue uphill along this road to a point where it turns sharply to the right. Leave the road here and strike ahead through two gates and onto a grassy track that rises steeply past former colliery workings, with a fence to the immediate left side. This colliery, thought to be named Twotop Colliery after the adjoining hill, has long since ceased production. The mine was, however, linked by a gravity tramway down to the Hartside Road, close to the route of the present metalled telecommunications tower access road. Once past the area of the workings the gradient begins to ease and a gate is reached. From here the track is reasonably level as it passes to the north side of Fiend's Fell. It then rises up a short steeper section (with optional routes here) to reach a gate. Pass through the gate then veer left to a second that leads into the rear section of the car park for the Hartside Top café. Pass around the café to the viewing area which provides a panoramic view across the Eden Valley.

The Ricker Gill crossing

4 Turn left out of the front of the Hartside Café car park by the A686 road. Instead of walking along the road immediately turn off left onto a wide rough track which is signed as an 'off road' section of the National Cycle Network's C2C route. Drop steeply down to reach the A686 road once again. Cross over the road and pass through a gate signed *Public Bridleway Selah Bridge* onto a track that firstly provides access to a 'bothy' style dwelling. Once past the dwelling continue downhill along a grassy path of varying gradients and after about a quarter of a mile drop steeply to cross Ricker Gill on a short length of gravel causeway, with foot and cycle bridges. *[Note: There is an old semi-derelict bridge across the Gill that may be used, at risk, as an alternative.]*

The **Hartside Top Café** claims to be the highest café in England at 1904ft above sea level. The café and its surrounds are noteworthy for the fine views across the Eden Valley and into the Lake District and Scotland. The area is also a congregating point for motor cyclists and for cyclists on the C2C route.

View north from Selah Bridge

Public Bridleway to Selah Bridge.
This route, which passes near to
several castles, was thought to have
formed a part of the medieval 'Via
Regia' or 'Monarch's Highway'. This
would have been the route followed
by the monarch during travels around
the kingdom. Hence, it had to be safe
and of a reasonable standard, and
was used by medieval long-distance
traffic.

Once over the Gill continue uphill a short distance and pass
through a gate. The route now contours as a wide grassy track
then descends (passing through two gates) and passes by sheep
pens and a derelict farm building. It then continues downhill
and after a further third of a mile reaches the Hartside to Renwick
road at Selah Bridge. Keep ahead along the road, cross Selah
Bridge, then turn off left at the top of a short hill rise, onto a
track signed as a *Public Byway* to *Five Lane Ends*.

5 The unsurfaced track continues the descent and after
turning has a long straight section of about a third of a mile.
It then undulates a little before dropping down quite steeply
into a shallow valley. Upon reaching this valley, at a more open
triangular shaped enclosed area, turn off left at a 'dog' leg in
the track, close to a ford. Turn around to the left, through an
area that may be somewhat boggy and cross Swarthgill Beck to
reach the left of two gates which are set close together. Pass
through the gate then proceed along a grassy track that rises
diagonally up the side of the low hill on the right. The track
then passes across the top of this hill and descends, with a fence
on the right side, to reach a gate at the commencement of the
metalled road in Busk hamlet. Pass through the gate and proceed
along the road between the buildings of the hamlet. As the
road turns to the right turn off left beside farm buildings onto
a track signed as a *Public Footpath* to *Cannerheugh*.

6 Pass through three gates in quick succession in the vicinity
of the farm buildings and an adjoining paddock. After the third,
continue along the right side of a field to reach a further gate.
Once through, turn to the right through an angle of about 60°
then follow the right side of the next field turning leftwards at
its lower corner to reach a gate at a wall projection in the lower
side of the field. Pass through this gate and cross the left corner
of the next field to reach a stone wall stile.

Bridleway from Hartside to Selah Bridge

Busk hamlet

Climb over the stile, cross a fieldside track, then proceed ahead keeping to the left side of a telegraph pole to reach another stone wall stile at the further side. From the stile cross the next field, in the same direction as before and drop down and over another stile. Cross a footbridge over Eller Beck then continue ahead up the right side of the next field with the path eventually becoming a grassy track. Pass through a gate and continue along an enclosed track to reach the Renwick to Unthank road.

7 **Turn left along the road,** then after descending and crossing Crofton Sike, turn off right along the access road signed to *Unthank*. Shortly pass farm buildings and descend to a junction in the centre of the hamlet with the access road to the right signed as a *Public Footpath* to *Gamblesby*. Turn right and proceed along the road for a short distance, then turn off to the left, immediately in front of a farm gate. Continue downhill on a grassy track that skirts a dwelling and its garden. At the foot of the slope pass through a gate (or over a stone stile) and cross a bridge over Hazelrigg Beck.

8 **Continue uphill from the bridge** and through a gate ahead at the top of the rise. Follow along the right edge of a field with a stone wall on the right side, then just after a shallow right bend in the wall climb over a stile, set in the wall (adjoining a gate), into the adjoining field. Continue then in the same direction as before, with the stone wall now on the left side. From where the wall bends to the left at a shallow angle continue ahead towards houses, to reach a kissing gate at the field boundary. Once through the gate pass along a short stretch of enclosed path and over a wall stile onto the Unthank to Gamblesby road. Turn right, along the road as it enters Gamblesby village, shortly reaching the green area and cross roads at the centre of the village and the end of the walk.

Unthank hamlet was originally a group of thatched dwellings surrounded by a wall, to keep out Scottish raiders. The name means a 'squatter's holding' or 'land held without consent'. The original settlement was at some distance from the present as the Black Death hit the original in 1597.

History, antiquities and riverside paths in the Eden valley.

The walk begins at Glassonby green. It leaves the village to the south and follows tracks and paths to Little Salkeld via the stone circle of Long Meg & her Daughters. It then turns north, alongside the Settle-Carlisle Railway and the River Eden and passes by Force Mill Weir, Lacy's Caves and Eden Bridge to reach Kirkoswald. It returns to Glassonby across field paths, passing by Kirkoswald Castle and the memorial at Old Parks to 'Romany of the BBC'.

St Michael and All Angels Church is in a parish named after a lost village. **Addingham** was an Anglo-Saxon settlement on the banks of the River Eden a little to the west. During the 14th Century the river changed its course and washed the village and original Medieval church away. The church has a number of interesting features including an Anglo-Saxon hammer-head cross and a Viking hog-back tombstone.

The Walk

1 Commence the walk from the green and with your back to the bus shelter proceed uphill and south along the road beside the green. From the top of the green continue between dwellings and shortly after leaving the village turn right, just past a barn onto a metalled access road. Follow along this road for the short distance to reach St Michael and All Angels Church, Addingham. Pass by the church and a 'Byway' sign onto a grass centred track and continue ahead to reach a signed path 'T' junction. Leave the junction along the path signed to *Long Meg* and after a short distance turn sharply left onto an enclosed tree and hedge lined path.

After about a third of a mile from the junction pass through a gate (or over a stile) onto a farm access track. Continue ahead and gently uphill along this track. Pass by a farm pond, through a gate and then Longmeg farmstead to reach the Bronze Age stone circle of Long Meg & her Daughters.

Glassonby

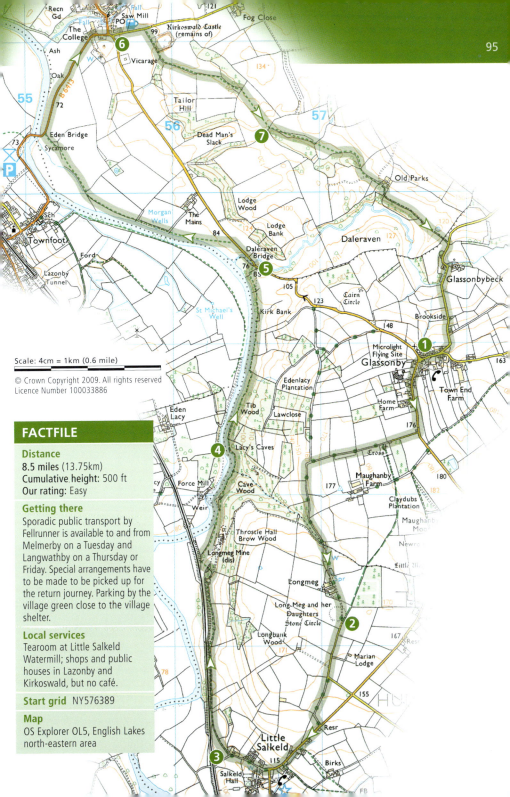

95

Scale: 4cm = 1km (0.6 mile)

© Crown Copyright 2009. All rights reserved
Licence Number 100033886

FACTFILE

Distance
8.5 miles (13.75km)
Cumulative height: 500 ft
Our rating: Easy

Getting there
Sporadic public transport by
Fellrunner is available to and from
Melmerby on a Tuesday and
Langwathby on a Thursday or
Friday. Special arrangements have
to be made to be picked up for
the return journey. Parking by the
village green close to the village
shelter.

Local services
Tearoom at Little Salkeld
Watermill; shops and public
houses in Lazonby and
Kirkoswald, but no café.

Start grid NY576389

Map
OS Explorer OL5, English Lakes
north-eastern area

2 Leave the stone circle along the same track which now becomes a metalled road. Continue along this road, across a cattle grid. When it turns sharply left continue ahead onto a grass centred track. Turn left with this track after about 250 yards to reach a 'T' junction with the Glassonby to Little Salkeld road. Turn right, along the road and drop downhill into Little Salkeld village. Where the road turns left, upon reaching the village green, continue ahead onto an access road. Keep the village green to the left and houses to the right and follow this road gently downhill to reach a junction just past the last buildings in the village. At this junction a private concrete road is signed *Public Footpath: Lacy's Caves* and *Daleraven Bridge*.

3 Proceed along the concrete road with the Settle-Carlisle railway on the left side. After nearly half a mile a turning area is reached, beside a bridge over the railway. Continue ahead here with the track signed to *Daleraven Bridge*. Look out for a brick, ground level, schools sculpture project on the left

Long Meg and her Daughters is the 3rd largest stone circle in England, after Avebury and Stanton Drew. It is composed of a large ellipse shaped ring of 59 light coloured porphyritic stones (the daughters) measuring 300 x 360 feet, and Long Meg, a large 12ft high outlying red sandstone pillar. On Long Meg there are some Bronze Age spiral carvings. A legend suggests that if Long Meg was damaged, she would begin to bleed. The relationship of Long Meg to the circle suggests the possibility that it may have been used to sight the midwinter sun.

Local folklore suggests that the stones were a coven of witches. They were celebrating their sabbath when a magician found them at it and turned them into stone. It is said that if the circle is moved or destroyed terrible misfortune (perhaps in the form of a ferocious storm) will fall upon those responsible. In 1725 Colonel Lacy of Salkeld Hall made an attempt to uproot and use the stones for mile posts. As the work began, however, a fierce storm blew up and the workmen fled believing the druids were angry at the desecration of the circle.

Lacy's Caves. In the late 18th Century Lieutenant Colonel Samuel Lacy had a batman (British Military Officer's Orderly) who had deserted the army. Instead of handing the servant over to the military he gave him the task of hewing caves out from the red sandstone beside the River Eden. The caves came to be used for entertaining guests

Longmeg mine was first opened in the 19th Century as a quarry, then mine for alabaster (or gypsum). This venture closed in 1915. It then re-opened in 1925 to recover or mine anhydrite by the company that eventually became British Gypsum. This venture closed in 1976.

which depicts places of interest in the Eden Valley. Continue for a short distance further to a derelict building on the right. Just past this building reach a gate across the track, by a junction and turn left down a short length of concrete access, signed to *Daleraven Bridge*. At a further gate turn sharp left, onto a cinder path, again signed to *Daleraven Bridge*. Pass by an electricity sub station then turn sharp right, with the path, and continue between fencing, into woodland. The path then continues along the top edge of a wooded embankment, amongst the faint remnants of the Longmeg mine structures. To the left the Eden Lacy Viaduct of the Settle-Carlisle Railway will be seen through the trees, then the path will turn a little, close to the Force Mill weir on the river (a steep 'dead end' path drops down to the weir at this point). Continue along the path, which is now close to the River Eden. Drop down some rough steps and over footbridges and shortly reach the junction with the entrance route to Lacy's Caves at the foot of a steep uphill section. A visit to the caves should be made from this point along the path to the left, before returning to the junction.

4 **From the junction proceed up the steep slope** and over the top of the caves. Descend again and continue alongside the river. The path passes beside cleared woodland and then has a significant section of board walk in Tib Wood, before reaching a stile at the edge of the woodland. Climb over the stile, then a second a little later. Cross a footbridge and then a third stile, all close to the river bank. The path then rises steeply to avoid an area of land slippage. Keep parallel with the river, but at the higher level to reach a wooden stile that leads from pasture into cleared woodland. From the stile descend steeply to reach the Glassonby to Kirkoswald road at Daleraven Bridge.

River Eden near
Daleraven Bridge

5 Turn left, along the road for a short distance, to reach a gate on the left at the beginning of a public footpath signed to *Eden Bridge*. Once through the gate proceed ahead across a field towards the River Eden, then with the river on the left side continue along the top edge of the bluff to a gate in the far corner. Once through the gate continue along a grassy riverside access track to reach a gate and stile. From here the path moves away from the river along the left edge of a field. At the further corner pass through a gate, cross a bridge and continue along the left edge of the next field. A stile and gate are located at a point, some distance along the edge, close to a tree clump. Climb over the stile (or pass through the gate) into the field which is closer to the river. Ahead will be the Eden Bridge, built in 1762 Continue then along the right edge of this field and over a stile that leads onto the B6413 (Lazonby to Kirkoswald) road at the end of the bridge abutment. Turn right, along the road and after a distance of about half a mile enter Kirkoswald village beside the walls of 'The College' and access to St Oswald's Church. The road then reaches a junction with another road signed to *Glassonby* and *Alston*.

Kirkoswald castle was a mediæval fortress, built in the 11th Century by Randolph Engayn, just after the Norman Conquest. Over the years it was devastated and rebuilt several times following Scottish raids. A park was provided by Sir Hugh De Morville and in the 16th Century ditch defences were added. In the 17th Century it came into the hands of the Dacre family, along with the manor of Kirkoswald and Lazonby. Lord Dacre ordered the castle to be dismantled in 1688 and stone was then used in some of Kirkoswald's buildings.

St Oswald's Church has the unique feature of its bell tower being perched on a hill top about 200 yards from the Church itself. The bell was probably used to warn villagers of the approach of Scots raiders, as well as summoning them to Church. One of Kirkoswald's most notable buildings is the College, the name recalling the days when St Oswald's Church was a collegiate church. The two storied house was originally built in 1450 as a Pele Tower and converted into the college for priests in the 1520's. It had a short life ending with the Dissolution in 1547. It then became home to the Fetherstonhaugh family.

Kirkoswald

6 **Turn right at the junction,** then immediately left at a second which is signed to *Park House* and *Alston*. Proceed along this road for a little over 200 yards then turn off to the right at a gate and stile signed as a *Public Footpath* to *Glassonby*. Pass to the right side of Kirkoswald Castle to a further gate (and stile). Once through continue ahead towards the left side of a plantation. When level with the plantation veer left along a rising grassy path which is set into a low hillside. Upon reaching a gate ahead don't go through but sidestep to the left and continue along the right edge of the existing field to reach a pair of gates in the further corner. Turn right and pass through the left gate, onto an enclosed grassy track, with woodland now to the left. Upon nearing a pond pass through a further gate then skirt around the left side of the pond. Once past the pond pass through another gate into a field. Continue ahead along the length of this field towards woodland and upon nearing the far boundary drop down to a gate (and stile) at the far edge beside the woodland.

7 **Once through (or over) proceed** along the right edge of the next field and after a little over 100 yards climb over a stile in the right fence into the woodland. Once in the woodland continue ahead in the same direction as before and climb over another stile at the far edge. Cross a short gap to a gate and further stile. From this stile the path crosses an 'indenting' section of the pasture ahead to a further section of woodland. Due to some boggy areas close to a gill it may be necessary to skirt around to the right. Once across, the path then veers left and continues around the left edge of the woodland. It then rises gently uphill to a gate at the further extremity of the woodland. Pass through the gate and continue along the left edge of a field to another gate that leads into the farmstead area of Old Parks. Once through this gate a notice board to the right records the life of 'Romany of the BBC'. Continue through the farmstead and out onto the main metalled farm access road. Follow this road to reach the Renwick to Glassonby road after about a third of a mile. Turn right, drop downhill to Glassonby Beck, then continue uphill to reach a junction at the entrance to Glassonby village. Turn right and return to the village green and end of the walk.

Romany (Rev. George Bramwell Evens, 1884 to 1943), was a Methodist Minister, stationed for a time in Carlisle. He spent much of his spare time exploring the lower Eden valley with his wife Eunice, dog Raq (always a Blue Roan English Cocker Spaniel) and horse Comma. He became well known for the pioneering Children's Hour BBC programme 'Out with Romany' which, with 13 million listeners, paved the way for modern naturalist radio and television broadcasting. Romany visited Old Parks regularly for 22 years and his ashes were scattered on the small hillock where the nearby memorial bird bath is located.

Eden Bridge

A walk full of character with interesting riverside vistas and historic association.

FACTFILE

Distance
Full walk: 3 miles (5km)
Shorter walk: 2.5 miles (4km)
Our rating: Easy

Getting there
Langwathby: Regular rail service to the village from Carlisle or Appleby-in-Westmorland on Settle-Carlisle Railway. Otherwise there is a very intermittent bus service from Penrith operated by the Fellrunner. Car parking on roads around the village green **Edenhall:** Intermittent Fellrunner bus service from Penrith. Car parking at church car park and in village.

Local services
Shop, teashop at station, Eden Ostrich World and public house in Langwathby; Edenhall Country Hotel in Edenhall.

Start grid
Langwathby: NY568336
Edenhall: NY568321

Map
OS Explorer OL5, English Lakes north-eastern area

The walk starts from the village green in Langwathby, five miles north-east of Penrith on the A686 Penrith - Alston road. An alternative shorter option for the walk begins from St. Cuthbert's church car park at Edenhall village.

Much of the walk lies close to the River Eden where there are good riverside vistas. The surrounds of Edenhall Village, with its church and historic associations provide additional interest.

In wet weather some parts of the walk can be muddy and after prolonged heavy rain the river can be high and fast running. The walk can be done safely, however, in all but the most severe conditions of flooding.

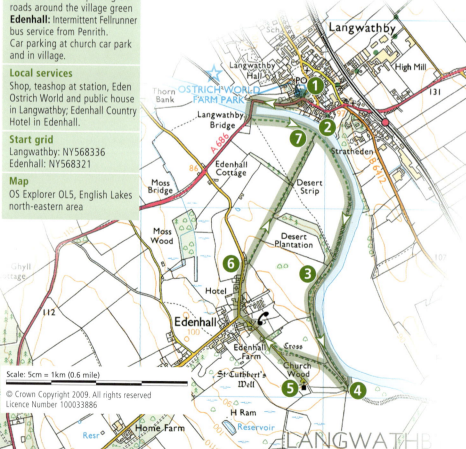

Scale: 5cm = 1km (0.6 mile)

The Walk:

1 Commence the walk on Langwathby village green and make for the A686 road exit towards Penrith at the junction close to the Shepherd's Inn. Continue along the right pavement beside a terrace of dwellings, then downhill beside a high retaining wall. Cross over the River Eden by the footway on the metal Bailey bridge. The original stone bridge was swept away in floods in 1968 after which this 'temporary' structure was installed. Once over the river turn left, cross the main road and pass through a kissing gate onto the riverside public footpath signed to *Edenhall*. Follow the path close to the river, along the left edge of a field. At the far corner of this field there is a junction of paths and another signpost.

Langwathby village green

Langwathby bridge

2 Continue, alongside the river on the path directed as *Edenhall and Church – Along River Bank*. After about half a mile the path reaches a kissing gate by woodland. Pass through the gate and follow the path up some steps away from the water's edge. The path continues alongside a field fence on the right and a line of beech trees on the left. You soon reach two carved stone seats which were sculptured as 'Eden Benchmarks' to provide a panoramic view across the Eden to The North Pennines. *[Note: the viewpoint may be a little obscured by tree growth]* Cross Fell, the highest point on the Pennine Way is the dominant hill with Great Dun Fell to it's right on which rests the Civil Air Traffic Control 'golf ball' radar dome.

3 The path now continues for some 300 yards, passes the end of a stone wall and descends via stone steps to a clear path above the river bank. This is the original Lady's Walk. Ladies were brought to one end of the walk in a carriage to promenade and be picked up at the other end. Eventually a small diversionary path can be taken which leads to and from a seat conveniently sited by the river. The main track follows the line of the retaining wall to reach a further kissing gate.

The seats, by Vivien Mousdell -called 'South Rising' -are one of the **Eden Benchmarks**, a series of sculptures placed at strategic points in the Eden Valley. Water fowl can often be seen from here.

The River Eden from Lady's Walk

View from St Cuthbert's church across the Eden to Cross Fell

The **Plague Trough** was a stone basin, filled with vinegar, into which plague victims put coins to pay for food brought by locals. The trough and the three steps leading up to it were discovered built into a wall which ran from here along the east side of nearby St Cuthbert's Church. The trough was removed and the cross erected in its place when the wall was taken down and used to build the retaining wall along the side of Lady's walk on the orders of Lady Musgrave of Eden Hall.

4 Go through the gate then turn sharp right, up a slope and follow a clear track across farmland to reach a gate which leads onto the access road to Edenhall Church. Here there is an old cross which was erected in the 1870's on the site of a 'plague trough'. Turn left, along the road and after about 200 yards reach a car park and access to St. Cuthbert's church. It is well worth looking inside the church and, in Spring, at the churchyard daffodil display.

5 From the church car park proceed back along the access road, pass by the old cross and continue straight on through the large stone gate posts at East Lodge into the village of Edenhall. The Musgrave Coat of Arms, which consists of six circles in a shield, appears on many houses in the village. Turn right at the road junction beside the bus shelter opposite the war memorial. Pass the Edenhall Country Hotel and continue as far as the playground and swings, adjacent to the former school on the right hand side of the road.

6 At this point turn right, off the road onto a track, signed to *Langwathby and The River Eden*. Pass through a gate and follow along the right edges of two adjacent fields. En route, drop downhill pass by a long narrow strip of sheltering trees and through a second gate, to reach the river bank at a signed junction of paths.

7 Turn left and retrace your steps along the river bank to Langwathby Bridge. Cross the main road and turn right, over the bridge and along the roadside pavement. Once again reach the village green and the end of the walk.

St Cuthbert's church is named after the tradition that the Jarrow monks, fleeing from the Vikings in the late ninth century, brought St Cuthbert's body here briefly during its seven year tortuous journey to Durham. The church contains the tombs of the Musgraves, owners of Eden Hall (demolished in 1934) for centuries. A treasured possession of the family was the 'Luck of Eden Hall', a 13th Century goblet of Syrian glass brought to Edenhall by a Musgrave returning from a Crusade. It was given to the Victoria and Albert Museum in London when the estate was broken up.

Shorter walk:

Commence the walk from the car park beside St Cuthbert's Church in Edenhall. The walk then follows the directions given in paragraphs 5 and 6 above. Once the signed junction of paths is reached beside the bank of the River Eden (point 7) turn right and follow the route described in paragraphs 2, 3 & 4 above, to return to the church and car park.

An attractive Eden village: its by-pass, its Moss and tranquil riverside paths.

FACTFILE

Distance
5 miles (8.25km)
Cumulative height: 269ft
To and from Acorn Bank:
2 miles (3km)
Our rating: Easy

Getting there
Public transport from Penrith or
Appleby 2-3 hourly (Bus route
563). Car parking on minor roads
around Temple Sowerby village
green.

Local services
Inn and restaurant in Temple
Sowerby. Tearoom at nearby
National Trust Acorn Bank (March
to October only) and Hazel Dene
Garden Centre in Culgaith.

Start grid NY611271

Map
OS Explorer OL19, Howgill Fells
& Upper Eden Valley

This is a walk which explores the banks of the River Eden,
with fine distant views of the North Pennines and the
Eastern Fells of the Lake District. It starts from the village
green in Temple Sowerby, a village located about half way
between Penrith and Appleby-in-Westmorland. In 2007 the
village began to benefit from the opening of its long
awaited by-pass for the A66 Trunk road.

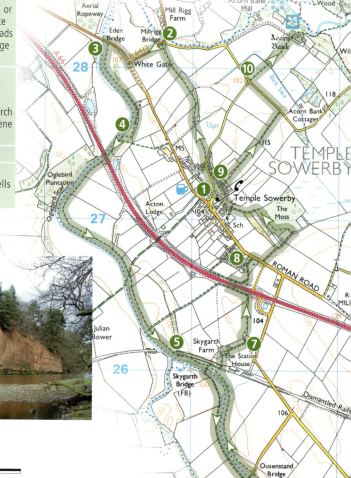

Eden Cliffs, near Temple Sowerby

Scale: 4cm = 1km (0.6 mile)

The Walk

1 With your back to the church commence the walk from the road junction close to the village green play area. Follow the main route across the length of the green, towards the north. Just past a junction with a road from the left turn off left, through a gate, onto a Public Footpath signed to *Millrigg*. Cross a field ahead, around the right flank of a grassy mound, then pass through a gate on the far side. Pass to the left of a compound containing Water Authority filter beds. Follow the fence line on the right side and climb over a stile near the next field corner. Cross the next three fields, with stiles between, keeping parallel to the fence which is a little way to the right. After the third such field bear right from the stile and continue, with the stream close by to the right, to reach a stile (and gate) at the B6412 road.

2 Turn left upon reaching the road. *[A short detour right to the Crowdundle Beck Bridge will reveal the letters C and W in the stonework at the centre of the parapet. Crowdundle Beck forms part of the old boundary between Cumberland and Westmorland].* Walk along the road to the T junction with the old A66 road (now renumbered B6412), then turn right and downhill along that road for about 200 yards towards its bridge over the River Eden. Cross over the road, then turn off left, over a stone step stile set in the bridge approach parapet, onto a Public Footpath signed to *Kirkby Thore*.

Eden Bridge near Temple Sowerby

Temple Sowerby village green

Oglebird Scar

'Red River'. Expressive of the Eden river valley geology the stepped slabs of Lazonby Sandstone represent the contours of the landscape and its light and shade, pattern, shape and form. The spheres, reminiscent of gigantic pebbles in a fast moving stream, are a powerful evocation of the river and its energy but also, like hugely magnified grains of sand, recall the origins of sandstone in the shifting sand dunes of Triassic Cumbria.

3 **From the stile follow alongside the River Eden** through a rather fine riverside meadow. Here there are views back to the Cross Fell range in the North Pennines. Pass through a gate at the far end then rise up along a field edge to a further gate. This leads into a green path that is squeezed between a residential property and a riverside cliff edge. Exit the enclosed path through another gate onto a high ledge, set above the river, with a fence to the left side. *[Here, on a clear day, there is a superb view from above the right-angled bend in the river. This includes the Lake District's Eastern Fells, with the High Street range coming into view]* Continue along the ledge and pass through a gate to reach Victoria Brailsford's sandstone sculpture 'Red River'. *[This is the fourth of ten 'Eden Benchmark' sculptures, which also function as seats, placed on footpaths along the length of the River Eden by the East Cumbria Countryside Project to mark the new Millennium]*

4 **Continue along the ledge,** then at the point where the left fence veers away, turn steeply downhill to the right onto a river bank meadow path close by the water's edge. Climb over a stile, pass beneath the A66 Temple Sowerby by-pass and climb over another stile. *[At this point there are high sandstone cliffs, known as Oglebird Scar, on the opposite side of the river. The Scar is a nesting place for wild birds]* Continue along the river bank, with the sandstone cliffs of the Scar on the far side. Once over the next stile follow the river bank as it turns around to the left to eventually reach another stile at the further extremity of the riverside meadow.

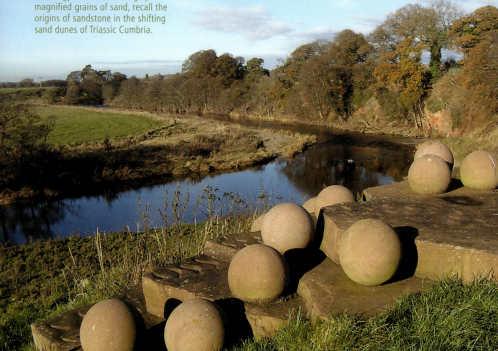

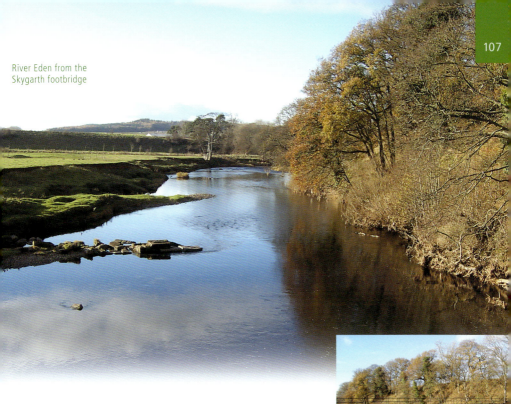

River Eden from the
Skygarth footbridge

Climb over this stile and continue through a section of rough
riverside grassland with a steep embankment to the left side.
Pass through a gate, near where a further path comes in from
the left, then shortly after climb over a stile into a field. Continue
along the right side of the field and after a further stile, beside
the next field, but separated off by a wire fence. The path then
passes beside the Skygarth Viaduct abutment of the former
Eden Valley railway before reaching a further stile.

Skygarth footbridge

5 Climb over the stile and then veer slightly left up a grassy
bank, close to the line of the former railway. Once at the top
of the rise follow along a fence line to the right to reach a gate
on the right and an enclosed path. Pass through the gate and
descend, through trees, to Skygarth footbridge across the River
Eden. Cross the footbridge then turn left and pass beside a
fisherman's sheltered seat. Continue then along a grassy track
beside the river to reach a gate and stile. The track then passes
along the edges of four fields, separated by stiles and gates, to
reach the Temple Sowerby to Morland road through a final gate.
Turn left at the road and cross over the River Eden a second
time, by Ousenstand Bridge.

Eden Valley railway. This rail line
ran from NE England over Stainmore
Summit, via Kirkby Stephen and
Appleby, to join the West Coast Main
Line just south of Penrith. The line
closed in the early 1960's. On the
opposite side of the river at this point
the River Lyvennet flows into the Eden.

6 Once over the bridge turn left, off the road, and climb
over a stile onto a Public Footpath signed to *Temple Sowerby
and Eden Bridge*. Proceed along the length of a narrow riverside
meadow and climb over a further stile at the far right side. From
the stile continue in the same direction as before, climb over a
further stile and follow along the river bank towards a riverside
woodland.

Former railway station

En route it is necessary to cross a small stream, close to its entry to the river, before veering right and rising up a grassy track between trees to reach an upper meadow. Once in this meadow a ramped path will be visible on the further side, with a gate at the top. Make towards this gate which leads to a bridge over the former Eden Valley railway. The former Temple Sowerby railway station will also be visible across the meadow. Cross the bridge, pass through a further gate and continue ahead towards the farmstead of Skygarth Farm. Upon reaching the buildings turn right, around the outside of the buildings, to reach the main metalled farm access road.

7 Turn right, onto the access road and proceed gently downhill to a right bend in the road. At this point turn off sharply left to reach a stile. Climb over the stile, veer to the right and proceed up the right side of a field towards the Temple Sowerby by-pass, which is visible. Climb over a stile to reach an enclosed track. Turn left, along the track, then turn right and pass beneath the by-pass through a subway. At the far side turn right, along another enclosed track, and continue gently uphill to reach a field beside a stone barn structure. Turn left at the barn, along a short section of field boundary and climb over a stile onto an enclosed access track that passes between dwelling curtilages. Turn right, whilst on the track, and shortly reach the former A66 road.

8 **Turn right, along the road,** then cross over onto a metalled access road, signed as *Public Footpath via The Moss*. Proceed along this access for about 350 yards by which point it will be passing woodland on the left side. Turn off left, down a woodland path, immediately to the left side of a disused brick storage building. Follow the path through 'The Moss' woodland, turning firstly to the left and shortly after to the right, then continue straight across the woodland. At the far side, the path (which may be overgrown) then bends a little before reaching a stile at the woodland edge. Climb over the stile, followed by a second stile. Pass beside a paddock then veer right, along a grassy access path, to reach a gate by dwellings in Temple Sowerby. Pass through the gate and turn right, along a road that leads past dwellings and the church to reach the village green and the end of the walk.

Additional walk to and from Acorn Bank:

9 **From the road junction,** again with your back to the church, go uphill beside the village green playground towards terraced dwellings. Cross over the upper level road onto a track that passes between the two terraced rows. A sign that reads *Public Footpath – Newbiggin Road* may be visible on the left side of the track. Pass through a gate at the end of the track, to the rear of the dwellings, into a long field. Veer left and continue along the left side of the field to reach a further gate at the far end. Once through this gate continue along the left edge of the next field to a further such gate that leads onto the Temple Sowerby to Newbiggin Road. Turn left, along the road, and after about 300 yards reach a road junction.

10 **Turn right, off the road,** through a gate onto a field path signed as a *Public Footpath to Newbiggin*. Ahead will be seen Acorn Bank house. Proceed ahead, across a field and drop down to cross Birk Sike by a further gate. Once through the gate continue uphill and pass beside some trees to reach a gate in the field boundary, just to the left of the house. Pass through the gate and after a few yards reach the main metalled access road to Acorn Bank. Turn right, cross a cattle grid and pass through the wrought iron entrance gates to the property. Once the National Trust gardens and tea room have been visited the route can be retraced back to Temple Sowerby.

Acorn Bank

Villages of the East Fellside and countryside in the shadow of Cross Fell

This walk utilises field paths between the three East Fellside villages of Skirwith, Kirkland and Blencarn. It also explores the North Pennines foothill country of Cross Fell from where extensive views across the Eden Valley can be gained. Part of the walk lies along the route of the historic 'Maiden Way' Roman Road, whilst another section keeps close to the shore of Blencarn Lake, one of the newest lakes in Eden. The walk starts from the frontage to St John's church in Skirwith, beside the rather elongated village green that borders Skirwith Beck.

Skirwith

The Walk

1 Commence the walk from the car park in front of the church. Turn right, out of the car park and after a very short distance veer off left and downhill along a metalled access road. As the road turns sharply left at the foot of the slope veer off to the right across grass to a wooden footbridge across Skirwith Beck. Cross over the bridge and turn right onto a grassy path. Within a short distance veer off left and proceed diagonally uphill to reach the Skirwith to Kirkland road and turn right. Proceed along the road, out of the village, rising gently towards Kirkland and Cross Fell. After about half a mile turn off left onto a metalled farm access road which is signed as a *Public Footpath* to *Ousby Townhead or Bankwood*.

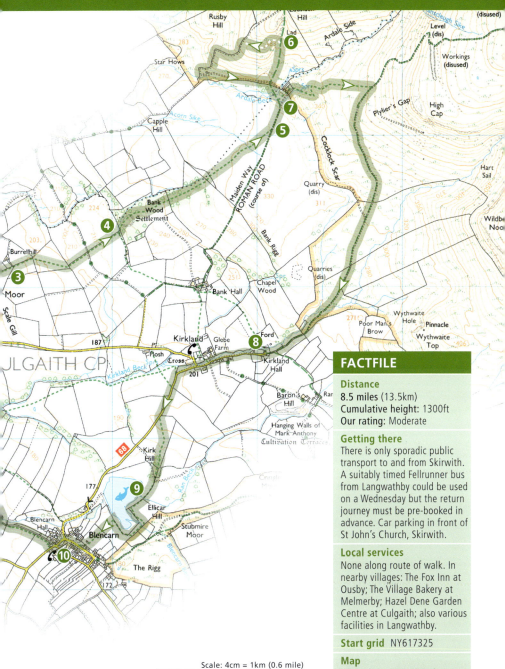

FACTFILE

Distance
8.5 miles (13.5km)
Cumulative height: 1300ft
Our rating: Moderate

Getting there
There is only sporadic public transport to and from Skirwith. A suitably timed Fellrunner bus from Langwathby could be used on a Wednesday but the return journey must be pre-booked in advance. Car parking in front of St John's Church, Skirwith.

Local services
None along route of walk. In nearby villages: The Fox Inn at Ousby; The Village Bakery at Melmerby; Hazel Dene Garden Centre at Culgaith; also various facilities in Langwathby.

Start grid NY617325

Map
OS Explorer OL31, North Pennines, Teesdale & Weardale

2 **Proceed along the access road** and where the metalled road turns sharply left continue ahead onto an unsurfaced track. Cross a cattle grid (with adjoining gate) and continue along the track which turns several times, descends and rises. After a distance of about a quarter of a mile from the cattle grid the track passes by then reaches the entrance drive on the left for the property Burrellhill. Pass across the head of the driveway to reach a gate.

3 **Pass through the gate** and proceed along the left edge of a field to reach a further gate. Once through veer right and cross the next field at an angle of about 45° from the left wall. At the far side of the field climb over a stone wall stile which is positioned mid way along the field edge. Once over, continue along the left edges of two fields, separated by a gate beside a cross track. At the further left corner of the second field climb over a wall stile into Bank Wood. *[The footpath cuts across the ancient settlement in Bank Wood. Circular mounds can be traced and walked on]*

4 **Veer left, from the stile** then after a short distance veer right and proceed uphill on a grassy track that curves gradually to the right through ancient deciduous woodland. Pass through the circular mounds of an ancient settlement and continue (turning a little) by following the direction of yellow signs fixed to trees shortly reaching the right corner of a fenced enclosure. Rise gently uphill, keeping the enclosure fence on the left side to reach a gate. Once through, continue ahead and uphill over rough enclosed pasture, with the incised course of a sike over to the left side. At the upper edge of the pasture pass through a gate onto open rough grassy moorland. Continue ahead close to the line of the sike on an indistinct path that keeps rising gently in the same direction as before. The route fords the upper reaches of Acorn Sike then, after a further 200 yards, reaches a shallow junction with the grassy route of the Roman Road 'Maiden Way'.

Skirwith to Burrellhill

5 **Veer slightly left onto Maiden Way** and follow this route a short distance further across the moorland. Drop down steeply and cross boggy ground by a ford to reach a signed path junction in the valley of Ardale Beck. Turn left at the junction onto the Public Bridleway path signed *Maiden Way - Hartside* and pass to the left of scrubby trees in the valley bottom before reaching the bridge across Ardale Beck. After crossing the bridge proceed ahead to reach a wall gate. Pass through the gate then proceed ahead to the foot of the steep uphill path up Lad Slack. Go to the foot of a rounded mound (probably made up of mine or quarry waste) which is located at the foot of the Slack and proceed along a steeply rising path around the right side that leads up past a yellow 'waymark' post to the rear upper level of this mound. Continue then a further short distance, steeply up the centre of the Slack across hillocks, probably formed from mine waste. Turn off left, though, out of the Slack where these hillocks finish (about a third of the distance up the Slack), onto a small path that leads between the hills that form its left side. As soon as seems practicable turn left, off the path and climb the steep grassy slope to the top of the left of these hills. From the summit of this unnamed hill (1250ft) broad sweeping views can be gained of the Eden Valley and beyond, especially on a clear day.

The **Maiden Way** (the name thought to be derived from Mai-dun – the great ridge) was an isolated Roman road leading south from Bewcastle and across the central section of Hadrian's Wall at 'Carvoran'. The route crossed over the North Pennines from the South Tyne Valley to the Eden Valley at Kirkland, then on to Kirkby Thore, the Lune Gorge and Kirkby Lonsdale. Because of the gradients much of the route would not have been suited to wheeled transport. It is thought that the section across the North Pennines would have been used by gangs of packhorses transporting mineral wealth from Alston to swell the tribute extracted by the Romans.

The hilltop above Lad Slack

6 Turn to the right on the summit (with your back now to Lad Slack) and descend the gentle shoulder slope as far as a clear grassy track which will be reached in advance of a fence. Turn left, onto this track, and follow it quite steeply downhill, keeping the fence to the right side, turning from time to time. The path approaches the upper area of a disused lime kiln, and then passes downhill to the right. At a junction turn left along a path that then passes immediately below the mouth of the kiln. Keep along this path, with Ardale Beck now to the right side. After about a third of a mile the path returns to the gate used earlier near the crossing point of Ardale Beck. Turn right and pass through this gate, cross the Beck and make back to the nearby path signed junction visited earlier.

Helm Wind. The part of this walk which lies close to the North Pennines and Cross Fell is subject to the effects of the Helm Wind, the only named wind in the British Isles. This is a cold, dry, violent wind from the east which desiccates and scorches vegetation and which blows down the leeward slope of the Pennines and out into the Eden Valley.

7 Turn left at the junction on the path signed as a *Public Footpath* to *Cross Fell* and *Garrigill*. Pass through a gate then continue ahead across a paddock type holding area. Once through a second gate continue uphill along a rising grassy track. This track climbs steeply up the hillside with two very sharp bends and other lesser corners. As the gradient eases the track becomes less pronounced and it then continues straight up the hillside to reach a junction with the Kirkland to Cross Fell and Garrigill bridleway. The junction is about a third of a mile from the lower path junction near Ardale Beck. Upon reaching this junction turn sharp right, onto the bridleway, then proceed along it downhill to Kirkland. The distance along the bridleway is about one and a quarter miles and en route it passes through three gates, with a descent of about 600 ft. It eventually becomes an enclosed track and then reaches a turning head at the end of the metalled road in Kirkland.

8 From the turning head continue along the local road through Kirkland. Pass by St Lawrence the Martyr's Church to reach the village road junction. *[Note: A deviation can be made to visit the church by crossing the footbridge in advance of the junction and climbing over a stone wall stile into the churchyard Leave the churchyard by the main entrance and turn left to reach the road junction.]* Keep ahead at the junction, which is signed to **Blencarn, Dufton & Appleby** and continue uphill along the road for a little over 200 yards. Turn off left, through a gate, onto a Public Footpath signed to **Blencarn**. Proceed ahead from the gate across and gently down the field, gradually making towards the left fence. At the foot of the slope continue ahead to a stile at the entrance to woodland. Once over, keep ahead to the further end of the woodland, but take care not to trip into holes or burrows close to the route of the path. Climb over a stile on leaving the wood and continue downhill with a field boundary to the left side. Cross a footbridge then turn left and over a stile in the left fence. Blencarn fishing lake will now be to your right side.

Crossfell Corpse Road. The bridleway leading down to Kirkland is part of the former 11 mile long Corpse Road that led from Garrigill to Kirkland. This was the highest and wildest such road in England, reaching to a height of about 2500 ft.

Kirkland. 'Estate belonging to the church'. This small East Fellside village lies at the end of the Corpse Road from Garrigill. The church, dedicated to St Lawrence the Martyr is pre 13th Century in origin, yet most recently re-built, probably for the third time, in 1880.

Blencarn Fishing Lake

Blencarn: 'cairn or rock summit'. This village is another in the line of East Fellside villages sitting near the foot of the North Pennines' leeward slope. The village has a long attractive green alongside which is one of the few thatched dwellings remaining in Eden.

9 Make for the further diagonal corner of the field. The path follows along the right boundary fence but due to poor drainage closer to the lake this route is often waterlogged. At the further corner pass through a gate then cross a slab footbridge, into the next field. Make gradually towards the fence on the right and at the corner turn right with the fence. Keep alongside for about 100 yards with the lake just beyond, then turn sharp left near a gate in the fence. Continue up the shallow hillside to reach a gate set about half way along the upper field boundary. Pass through the gate and keep along the right side of the next field, with a garden to the right. At the far corner pass through a gate onto Blencarn village green and continue ahead to the village street.

10 Turn right, along the road to a junction, then left (signed to *Culgaith*), through to another road junction. Turn right, as signed to *Skirwith* and *Penrith* and after a few yards turn off right, over a wall stile, onto a pubic footpath signed to *Skirwith* and *Kirkland*. Pass along an enclosed length of path between dwellings and over a stile into a field. Continue to the further right corner of the field and over a stile into a second. Keep along the right side of this field and over a stile (or through a gate) at the further right corner. Once over turn left along an unmade track. Shortly turn right, with the track, cross over Blencarn Beck then turn left. Keep along the track as it gently rises uphill, becoming grassy, to reach a gate. From the gate the path then crosses straight over three fields, each separated by a gate and stile. After the third the path veers right and crosses a fourth to reach a further gate and ladder stile.

11 Climb over the stile and proceed ahead across the next field to reach a gate by a wall corner that appears to project into the field. Pass through the gate and continue along the left edge of the next field to a point where a yellow painted post stands alongside the wall. At this point veer off right across the field corner to reach a ladder stile. Once over, continue along the left edge of the next field as far as a stile ahead, by a gate that leads into an enclosed path. Proceed along this path between trees and thicket and over a further stile at the far end. Continue then along the left side of a pasture to reach a stile and gate that lead into an enclosed path.

12 Proceed along this path, with woodland on the right side and gradually descend for about a third of a mile to reach a footbridge across Skirwith Beck at the foot of the slope. *[Note: Parts of this path may be very muddy]* Cross the footbridge, then proceed ahead onto a grassy path and pass to the left of a dwelling. Keep a wall on the immediate left side and turn left at the wall corner along a path that leads back to the Skirwith Beck footbridge which was crossed at the beginning of the walk. Cross the bridge once again and continue uphill on the metalled driveway back to the Skirwith Church car park and the end of the walk.

Skirwith. 'A wood shared in common by a whole district'. This is one of a line of traditional attractive East Fellside villages that are linked by a series of local roads between Castle Carrock in the north and Warcop in the south. The village sits either side of the Skirwith beck along the top edges of the beck slopes.

Cross Fell & Great Dun Fell

A deeply incised wooded riverside path and the contrast of wide views across undulating countryside

FACTFILE

Distance
5.5 miles (8.75km)
Cumulative height: 350 ft
Our rating: Easy

Getting there
Public transport to and from
Kirkoswald is sporadic. Two buses
run from Penrith on a Saturday
(Route 133). Parking in the small
square or on adjoining streets in
the village.

Local services
Shop and public houses in
Kirkoswald but no café.

Start grid NY554412

Map
OS Explorer OL5, English Lakes
north-eastern area

The walk begins in Kirkoswald's cobbled central square. It then leaves the village on its east side through woodland and across meadows along the Raven Beck riverside path. From Park Head it rises up then follows undulating field paths from which wide scale views can be gained of the North Pennines and Eden Valley. Small hamlets are encountered and the route eventually drops steeply down through woodland to the Raven Beck, as it returns to Kirkoswald.

Weir on the
Raven Beck

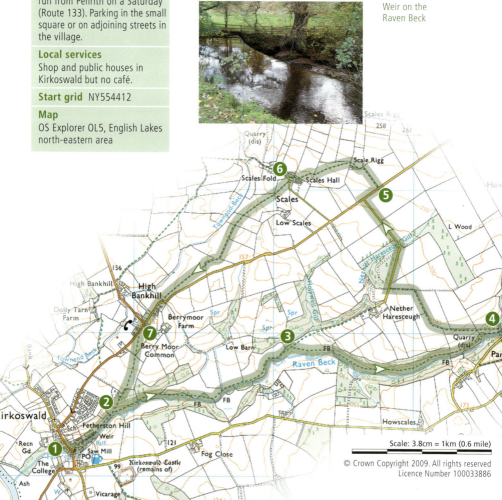

Raven Beck near Park Head

The Walk

1 Commencing the walk from the square, turn right and follow the main village street downhill for a few yards to a corner. Turn left into the residential street, Ravenghyll, signed on the left property wall as a *Public Footpath* to *Parkhead* and *High Bankhill*. Proceed along the metalled road, past houses and continue, when the metalling finishes, along an unsurfaced track to reach a gate. The track passes close to a former sawmill, the machinery for which was driven by water from Raven Beck. A water trough exists near the fence which led to the water wheel beside the mill. A little further on is a junction of water troughs where a small sluice could divert water to operate the sawmill. Beside the gate is a waterfall from where the trough flowed. Pass through the gate and continue, close to Raven Beck, along the lower level of a steep grassy pasture. At the end of the pasture pass through a further gate into woodland and shortly after reach a waymarked path junction.

2 Keep ahead at the junction onto the lower path close to the beck. *[Note: the path continues on beside Raven Beck for about 2 miles. Whilst several bridges are encountered it does not cross over the beck.]* Keep a look out for dippers. These black birds with a white breast are commonly seen on stones in the beck. Follow this path, with the beck generally close by on the right. After about a quarter of a mile a footbridge is passed, that crosses over the beck. Shortly after, reach a stile that leads out of the woodland into a broad, flat meadow. *[Note: This stile has a somewhat unusual 'user friendly' hand post.]* Once over the stile continue along the right edge of the meadow with beckside woodland to the right. On a clear day fine views of the North Pennines can be gained ahead from the meadow. Pass by a dilapidated suspension footbridge and a sturdy farm access bridge to reach a stile (and gate) at the end of the meadow. Continue along the short right side of a field, beside the beck and then along the right side of a further long field to a footbridge, stile and gate at the far end. Once over the stile continue ahead for 100 yards, with woodland on the left side, to a way marked path junction.

St Oswald's Church has the unique feature of its bell tower being perched on a hill top about 200 yards from the Church. The bell was probably used to warn villagers of the approach of Scots raiders, as well as summoning them to Church. One of Kirkoswald's most notable buildings is the College, the name recalling the days when St Oswald's Church was a collegiate church. The two storied house was originally built in 1450 as a Pele Tower and converted into the college for priests in the 1520's. It had a short life ending with the Dissolution in 1547, becoming home to the Fetherstonhaugh family, who previously lived at Kirkoswald Castle. The Castle is now a ruin, having become unused and had most of its material sold off in the C17th.

Autumn colours along the Raven Beck

3 Fork right at the junction (do not proceed uphill) and
continue along the length of a low meadow, keeping the beck
again close by to the right. At the end of the meadow pass
through a gate into woodland. From the gate the path winds
through beckside woodland for about half a mile. For much of
the length of this woodland there is a steep cliff on the left side
and a plantation of poplar trees (planted in 1985) on the flatter
beck side area through which the path goes. Walk fairly straight
on through the poplar trees and do not be tempted to cross the
wide bridge to the right over the beck with the 'No Entry' sign.
The valley gradually narrows and enters a short section of gorge
at the end of the poplar planting. The path then reaches a wall
stile at the end of the woodland. Climb over the stile then
traverse an open narrow beck side area with mature trees on
the steep bank to the left. Climb over two stiles, either end of
a further short constrained former quarry area. Continue along
the lower right side of a meadow to reach a stile and path
junction at the far end, close to the hamlet of Park Head.

4 Do not climb over the stile but turn sharp left onto a grassy lonning, set between a fence and a line of hawthorns. Climb uphill, away from the beck and after about 50 yards turn left, once again, as waymarked. Continue uphill along the lonning, still between hawthorns, to reach a gate at the top corner of the meadow. Pass through the gate and continue more gently uphill along the upper right side of a field. Pass through a second gate and keeping the wall to the right side turn right as the slope evens out. Pass through a third gate and keep on to a path junction at the field corner. Turn left at the junction, keeping within this field to reach a fourth gate at a local access road. To the left at this point is the farm property Nether Haresceugh. Turn right, onto the metalled road, and continue along for about a quarter of a mile to a 'T' junction with the Kirkoswald to Renwick road. Turn right and after a further 150 yards turn off left onto an access road signed as a *Public Footpath* to *Scales*.

5 Cross a cattle grid (adjoining gate) and proceed up the drive of the property Scale Rigg. Once the yard and turning area has been reached turn right, through a gate, into a field. Veer left and follow the left fence around to the rear of the property to reach a further gate. Once through this gate the farmstead of 'Scales Hall' will be in view across the left diagonal of the next field. Cross the field, in the direction of the property, to reach a further gate. Once through the gate continue, with an enclosed planted area to the left and cross a rough track to reach a stile. Climb over the stile into a paddock and turn right. Pass through a gate at the further end then cross a concrete farm apron area, between buildings. Turn left and leave the apron area through a gate onto the metalled Scales access road. Cross the road diagonally right to a stone wall stile beside a Public Footpath sign to *Kirkoswald.*

Nether Haresceugh is a typical fortified house, designed to repel the Scots and cattle thieves. The property is noteworthy for its 'Luck'. This is a small glass bowl of dark claret with a white rim. Lucks are connected with Celtic and Scandinavian 'magic cauldrons' – precursors of the holy grail legends.

Scale Rigg

Footpath between Scales and High Bankhill

6 From the stile veer slightly left and cross a field to a stile set in a shallow field corner. Once over the stile continue in the same general direction as before. Pass over a raised mounded part of the field to reach a pair of stiles in the further fence line. Once across, continue over the next field to a metal gate that leads into a green enclosed lonning. From the gate traverse the length of the lonning to reach a stile (and gate). Once over, turn right and cross a small section of field to a wall stile set in an otherwise fenced boundary. Once over the stile continue ahead and at the further lower end of a field reach a wall stile (and gate) that leads onto the Kirkoswald to Renwick road. Veer right, along the road, into the hamlet of High Bankhill and shortly reach a 'T' road junction with the B6413 road. From the 'T' junction one of the few surviving Cumbrian thatched dwellings can be viewed along the road to the right.

7 From the junction continue ahead as directed towards Kirkoswald and Lazonby and after 100 yards turn off left, through a gate, onto a Public Footpath signed to *Kirkoswald*. Veer right and cross to a wall stile in the further right corner of a field. From the stile continue, in the same direction as before, keeping parallel with the left boundary of the field and making gently downhill towards a projecting corner of woodland. Pass to the immediate right of the corner and shortly after reach a stile that leads into the woodland. Once over the stile continue steeply downhill, through the woodland, on a winding path that crosses a small ravine and eventually reaches a path junction, which was visited on the outward section of the walk, close to Raven Beck. Veer right at the junction to shortly reach a gate that leads out of the woodland. Continue, by retracing your steps back into Kirkoswald to reach the cobbled central square, once again, and the end of the walk.

Kirkoswald is a picturesque once-thriving market town, containing some fine Georgian buildings and a small cobbled market place. The village derives its name from the Church of St Oswald. Oswald was the King of Northumbria who, according to legend, toured the pagan North with St Aidan in the 7th Century. The market moved from the market square to Lazonby station, following the opening of the Settle-Carlisle Railway in 1876.

Walking to the
North & West
of Penrith

ramblers
at the heart of walking

Field paths in the Communication Corridor on the northern fringes of Penrith

The walk commences from Penrith Market Square. The Market Square lies in the centre of the town and contains the 1861 Musgrave Monument Clock Tower. The walk passes out of the town via Townhead into the low lying area in the vicinity of Thacka Beck that forms the transport corridor to the north of the town. Upon reaching the River Petteril near Catterlen it then turns and passes close to Newton Rigg College before reaching Gilwilly. It returns to Penrith town centre via pedestrian routes through Castletown and Brunswick Square.

FACTFILE

Distance
5.5 miles (9km)
Cumulative height: 150ft
Our rating: Easy

Getting there
Regular public transport to Penrith from Carlisle, Kendal, Keswick and several towns and villages in Eden. Car parking in and near the town centre.

Local services
Several cafés, restaurants and public houses in Penrith.

Start grid NY515301

Map
OS Explorer OL5, English Lakes north-eastern area

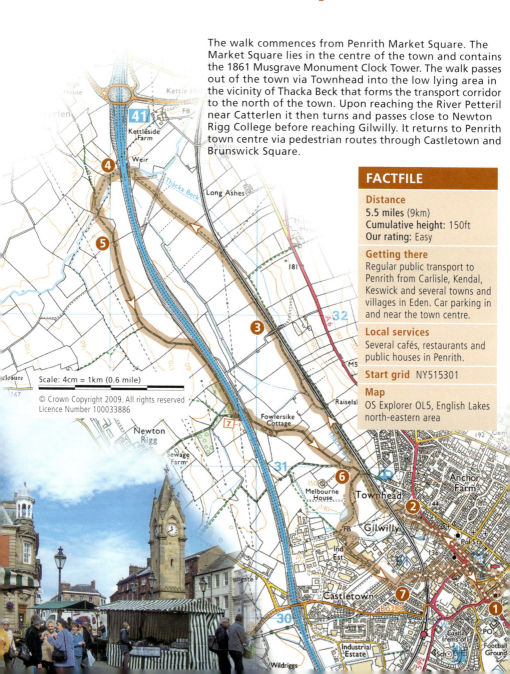

Scale: 4cm = 1km (0.6 mile)

Stricklandgate, Penrith

The Walk

1 Locate St Andrews Church Square which leads in an easterly direction from the Market Square between The National Westminster and Barclays banks. Proceed along the pedestrian route and pass to the left side of the church and churchyard. At the foot of the lane turn left at De Whelpdale Lane and continue along the left pavement to reach the zebra crossing over Burrowgate. Cross over, turn right, then left along a short pedestrian alley between the Co-op store and the Grey Goat public house. Cross another zebra crossing then turn left, along the right pavement of Albert Street. Keep on this pavement, cross over the bus station/car park entrance, the junction with Hunter Lane, pass the front of the Town Hall and cross over the junction with Portland Place. You will then be walking along Stricklandgate and after rising up a little will reach another zebra crossing by the shallow junction with Foster Street, to the left. The walk here is passing through Townhead, the northern entrance part of Penrith lying in the vicinity of the former A6 trunk route. Cross over and turn right, into Foster Street, then continue between houses along this narrow street to the point where it turns to the right to become Lark Lane.

? Turn left off the road along a path signed *Public Footpath Thacka Lane*. Pass through various gates as the path turns and drops down and under the West Coast Main Line. Once under the railway turn around to the right and continue to a stile at Thacka Lane. Keep the railway and bridge at this point on the right side and cross over the lane to a lineside path which lies between the railway embankment and Thacka Beck. Proceed along the path, which keeps alongside and within sight of the railway. Pass through two gates and a gateway and after about two thirds of a mile reach an overbridge of both the railway and the footpath. At this point the path passes through two gates beneath the bridge.

Penrith Church, dedicated to Saint Andrew, was built between 1720 and 1722 in the Grecian style. The earliest record of a church on the site is 1133 and the west tower of an older church was incorporated within the present. Within the church are two large brass chandeliers which were presented to the people of Penrith for resisting the 1745 Jacobite Rebellion. There are many interesting features in the church, including a plate to commemorate the bubonic plague, which killed many Penrithians in 1597-98. The church yard includes two antique monuments: 'The Giant's Grave' and 'The Giant's Thumb'. Their role and purpose is a mystery. One theory is that the 'grave' is associated with Owen Caesarius, King of Cumbria, who died in 937. The 'thumb' is the remains of a 10th Century Saxon Cross.

The property **Page Hall**, located on the left side of Foster Street was one of the childhood homes (for 10 years) of Samuel Plimsoll, MP and social reformer. Plimsoll devised the 1875 Merchant Shipping Act, which introduced the Plimsoll Line for ships.

In 1385, Bishop Strickland diverted **Thacka Beck** from the River Petteril to supply water to Penrith. The Beck, which is largely in an underground conduit as it passes through Penrith, flows from the River Petteril near Catterlen, to the River Eamont.

3 **From the bridge continue** immediately alongside the railway. Pass through two gates and after a further third of a mile reach a stile close to an electricity pylon. Once over the stile veer left, away from the railway, along a slightly raised straight embankment, to reach a stile. From the stile continue along the left edge of a field. This section of path crosses over two distinct raised lengths of mounding as it approaches the M6 Motorway. From the top of the second length of mounding veer right, to reach a gate at the field edge, set close to the River Petteril. Pass through the gate and continue ahead to reach an underpass of the M6, set immediately alongside the river. Pass beneath the Motorway to another gate at the further side.

4 **After leaving the underpass** proceed ahead to a stile, then cross a footbridge over the River Petteril. Veer left from the footbridge and keeping the river to the left side cross a riverside pasture to reach a second footbridge over the river. Cross over this bridge and veer right, beside the river to a gate. From this gate follow a short section of enclosed path, still beside the river, to a further gate that opens into a field. Once through this gate turn left and uphill, across the centre of the field, to pass between two electricity poles which will be visible at the top of the rise. From the poles continue a short distance to a gate which leads into an enclosed path.

Bridge over the River Petteril

5 **Turn right, along the path** and pass by a stone barn. Follow this path for approximately one mile as it rises up and then descends, to eventually come immediately alongside the M6 Motorway. The track finishes at a signed 'T' junction of tracks, alongside a motorway underpass. Turn left and pass beneath the Motorway along a track signed as a *Public Bridleway* to *Penrith*. Turn right, once through the underpass (signed here as C2C cycleway) and follow this track, passing by the property 'Fowlerside Cottage'. This track is metalled and after about half a mile from the underpass it passes some dwellings and descends to approach Thacka Beck and the Thacka Lane bridge at a point visited earlier in the walk.

6 Do not cross the Beck but turn sharp right, following around the wall of the field on the right to reach a gate. Pass through or beside this gate onto a grassy path. Continue along this path as it passes through a wooden gate and skirts to the left of a lake, eventually reaching Bowerbank Way on Gilwilly Industrial Estate. Turn left, along the estate road, then right into a cul-de-sac. Continue along an enclosed path from the end and after passing between industrial premises reach Gilwilly Road. Cross this road and pass between playing fields and allotment gardens.

7 Once past the playing fields turn left and cross road ends diagonally right onto an enclosed path with allotment gardens to the right side. Continue along this path, cross a footbridge over the West Coast Main Line and shortly reach a 'T' road junction. Turn left, then right to reach Brunswick Square. Pass around two sides of the Square to the far lower corner, then turn right along an enclosed path to reach Brunswick Road. Turn left, down Brunswick Road, then right at the pedestrian lights into Middlegate shopping street. Continue along this street and pass through the narrow section of the street to reach the Market Square and the finishing point of the walk.

The **M6 Motorway** through Cumbria was built and opened during the late 60's & early 70's. The section crossed by this walk is the 7 mile 'Penrith By-Pass' section. This section was opened in November 1968.

The **C2C Cycle route** is the most popular cycle route in Britain. It is 132 miles in length and links Whitehaven or Workington with Tynemouth or Sunderland.

Brunswick Square

FACTFILE

Distance
10.5 miles (17km)
Cumulative height: 800ft
Our rating: Moderate

Getting there
Parking on roadside close to village crossroads. There is no suitably timed public transport.

Local services
None in vicinity of walk. Closest are located at Greystoke, Mungrisdale and Unthank.

Start grid NY409358

Maps
OS Explorer OL5, English Lakes north-eastern area

Inglewood and Greystoke Forest landscape with viewpoints towards the northern Lakeland fells

The walk begins at the crossroads in the centre of Lamonby village, about 8 miles to the north-west of Penrith.

The walk is amongst the sparsely populated agricultural and forestry landscapes to the north west of Penrith. The paths walked are undulating and several provide sweeping elevated views of the northern Lake District and the Eden Valley. The paths in Greystoke Forest are permissive routes during daylight hours only and may be subject to restricted usage whilst 'off road' racing is taking place.

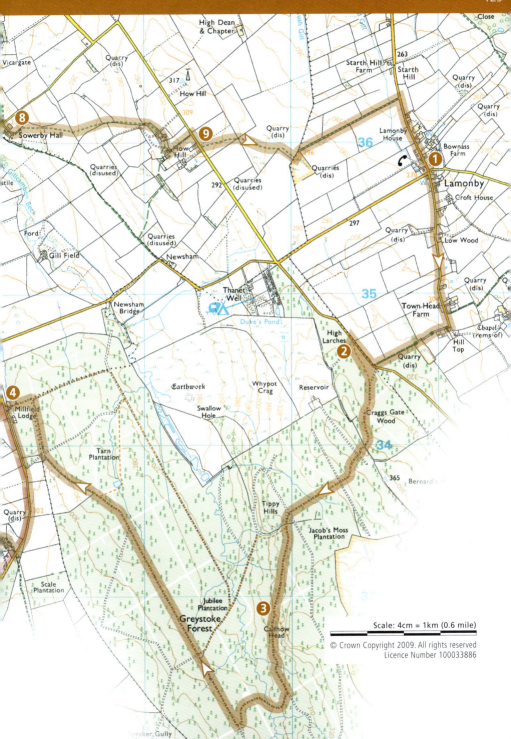

Scale: 4cm = 1km (0.6 mile)

The Walk

1 Commence the walk from the Lamonby village cross roads, along the narrow road to the south which has a *no through road* sign. Follow along this road for about two thirds of a mile to reach a track on the right, just in advance of a gateway where the metalling ends. Turn right, along this track, pass by some dwellings and continue beside field edges. Pass through three gates to reach the Greystoke to Millhouse road, up against Greystoke Forest. Turn right, along the road, for about 200 yards then left along a track signed *Forest Walk*. This leads into the eastern forest car park.

2 Cross the car park onto the signed forest path, which here provides red and blue arrowed signs and one which reads 'walkers welcome'. Proceed along the path to reach a vehicular forest track and turn right. Follow the track as it shortly rises up through Craggs Gate Wood and passes beside an old cleared quarry area. It then descends and after a straight section of about a quarter of a mile reaches a cross junction of tracks. Pass over this junction (the route veering left) and continue ahead. At a junction with a path to the right continue ahead on the track, signed *View Point*. After a further short distance the track reaches a junction on the left, signed *Viewpoint/Picnic Table*.

[This path may be followed uphill to the viewpoint at Calfhow Head, which provides good vistas to the south across the Lakeland Fells. From the viewpoint retrace your steps back to the track]

Walkers welcome and directional signs on forest tracks

3 Continue gently downhill along the track, from the 'viewpoint' junction. As the gradient eases the track rounds a very distinctive 'zig-zag' as it crosses a watercourse. After a further 200 yards turn right at a track junction. This new track curves gently around to the right, crosses a water course and then gently around to the left to reach another track junction at a large triangular shaped open area. Turn right, across the shorter side of this triangle and then right again to be faced with a long straight track stretching towards the horizon. Proceed along this mile long straight, ignoring any junctions, then remain on the track as it turns and after a further 200 yards reaches a junction with a waymarked path to the right. Keep ahead on the track at this junction and shortly rise gently uphill to reach a 'cross junction' of tracks. Cross over the junction (the route veering right) and after a further quarter of a mile reach another track junction. Turn left here, along the track signed to *Millfield*. Shortly pass through two gates and cross the small western Millfield Lodge car park for Greystoke Forest to reach the Millhouse to Mungrisdale road.

Greystoke Forest is a large privately owned productive forest which is home to a large number of Roe deer. The forest has a number of permissive way-marked circular walks. Regular use is now made of the Forest for off road car rallying.

Village green at Hutton Roof

4 **Turn left, along the road** for about two thirds of a mile to reach Scales Farm on the right. Turn right, along the farm access road, signed as a **Public Footpath**. *[Note: This will be the second access road reached at the farm]* Pass beside buildings and through a number of gates then turn left, with a track, between two barn buildings. Once through, turn right, off the track and up a rough bank to a stile beside a wall corner. Climb over the stile and drop immediately down a grassy bank ahead. Turn right at the foot and continue along a field edge with embankment trees to the right. Climb over a stile and continue ahead to a gate. Once through, veer slightly left across the next field to a gate in the further left corner. Pass through and along the right side of a narrow wooded enclosed area. At the further end continue along the right side of the next field, through a gateway and across another field to a ladder stile. From here veer slightly left and cross the next field to a gate that leads onto an enclosed grassy path. Follow this path, with some corners, and eventually pass through a gate onto the village street at Hutton Roof. Turn left, along the road and shortly come alongside the village green on the right.

5 **Pass by the green and village pond** then turn sharply right, off the road, onto a public footpath signed to *Stewart Hill*. Pass beside the pond and through a gate, cross a farm access and over a wall stile into a field. Proceed then gently downhill, along the left edges of three fields, separated respectively by a gate and stile/footbridge.

Meadow at Stewart Hill

Carrock Fell

Climb over a stile at the lower left corner of the third field, and turn left onto the local road at Stewart Hill. Continue along this road for about 150 yards and turn off right, in advance of the property 'Marks House' onto a signed *Public Footpath*. Climb over a stile and proceed along the left edges of two fields, separated by a stile. Climb over a stile at the further corner of the second, then drop down sharply left in the third to a gate. Pass through the gate onto the Berrier to Haltcliffe Bridge road and turn right.

6 Follow along the road for about 150 yards then turn off right onto a Public Footpath signed to *Bishopspot*. Climb over a stile, then turn left and over a second. Proceed then ahead, parallel with the road, towards the property 'Heggle Lane'. Pass through gates onto the drive of the property, turn right and pass between farm buildings, together with some more gates. Continue ahead, once through the farmstead, along a grassy track that curves gently to the right across the centre of a field, to reach a stile and footbridge at Heggle Sike. Once over the Sike, cross a field corner ahead, to a second stile and footbridge. Veer then very slightly to the right and rise uphill across the next field to reach a stile. Once over, continue ahead in the same direction as before to a further stile that is set close to the corner of a section of field boundary that protrudes into the field. From this stile continue ahead across rough pasture, moving gradually away from the right field boundary and towards the property 'Bishopspot' which will become visible ahead. Skirt around some earthworks to reach a stile set in the hedge of the property boundary. Once over proceed along a path and drive set between the dwelling and a garden. Once past the house and through a gate turn left to a stile that leads into a field. Turn right, once over the stile, and follow the right field edge, then over a further stile and ditch (no bridge) to reach, once again, the Millhouse to Mungrisdale Road.

Heggle Lane Farm

Sowerby Hall

St Kentigern's Church and well is
built at a place where St Kentigern is
said to have baptized converts. The
well is now dry, and is situated in the
churchyard wall. There was originally
a 12th century church, which was
enlarged in the 16th Century.

7 **Turn left, along the road,** for a few yards then right along
a track signed as a *Public Footpath* to *St. Kentigern's Church*.
Drop down through trees to a ford and footbridge across
Gillcambon Beck. Pass through a gate then rise uphill with St
Kentigern's Church on the left. Cut up to the left and through
a gate into the churchyard. Pass through and emerge at the
main gate onto the access road to Sowerby Hall. Proceed ahead
along the access road and once alongside Sowerby Hall veer off
left along a grassy track which is signed as a *Public Footpath*
to *How Hill*.

8 **Follow this track gently uphill** and over a stile into a field.
Veer right, across the field, to a stile in the further left corner.
Once over, cross a field corner at a fairly shallow angle to the
left boundary, to reach another stile along the further edge.
From this stile continue ahead but veer gradually towards the
right boundary and a gate in the further right corner. Follow
along the right edges of two fields, separated by a gate, then
through a gate and over a stile to enter woodland near How
Hill. Pass along the length of the woodland and over a stile
at the further left edge. Once over turn right to reach a farm access
road, then immediately right, through a gate into the farm yard.
Turn then left, through 180°, and out of the yard again through
a gate into a field. Veer right, around the left edge of some
barns to a gate set in the lower right corner of the field. Continue
along the right edge of the next field and out through a gate
in the corner onto a metalled driveway. Turn left and uphill
along the driveway, to a junction with the Johnby to Millhouse
road.

9 **Turn right, along the road,** for a few yards then off left, through a gate, onto a Public Footpath signed to *Lamonby Quarries*. Cross a field diagonally to a gate in the lower right corner. Once through, climb over the ladder stile that is set in the wall on the right. From here navigate around boggy land and proceed ahead across a right field corner to meet the wall again at a sharp corner (the wall turns through 270° within the field at this point). Continue then, with the wall on the immediate right, to reach a gate close to a corner of the field. Once through turn left, along the edge of former quarry land and through another gate onto a rough access track. Continue along this track for about half a mile, gradually descending, to reach the local road at Lamonby. Turn right, along this road to arrive at the Lamonby crossroads after a third of a mile and the end of the walk.

The valleys of the Ive and the Roe, a sculpture park, the distant ruins of a castle and a new rural settlement

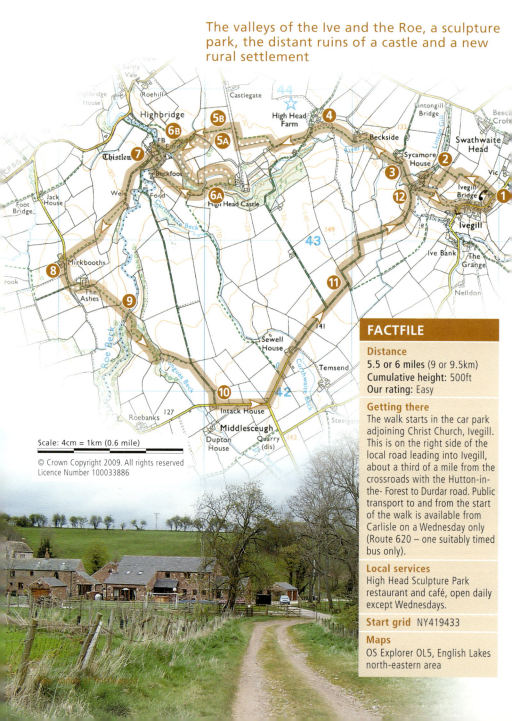

Scale: 4cm = 1km (0.6 mile)

© Crown Copyright 2009. All rights reserved
Licence Number 100033886

FACTFILE

Distance
5.5 or 6 miles (9 or 9.5km)
Cumulative height: 500ft
Our rating: Easy

Getting there
The walk starts in the car park adjoining Christ Church, Ivegill. This is on the right side of the local road leading into Ivegill, about a third of a mile from the crossroads with the Hutton-in-the- Forest to Durdar road. Public transport to and from the start of the walk is available from Carlisle on a Wednesday only (Route 620 – one suitably timed bus only).

Local services
High Head Sculpture Park restaurant and café, open daily except Wednesdays.

Start grid   NY419433

Maps
OS Explorer OL5, English Lakes north-eastern area

The walk begins in the car park beside Christ Church, Ivegill, about 11 miles to the north of Penrith.

The walk traverses the valley landscape of the River Ive, between Ivegill, High Head and Thistlewood. It provides the opportunity to visit the High Head Sculpture Park and also some paths opened up under the DEFR Conservation Walks scheme. From Thistlewood the route crosses farmland and the valleys of Roe and Tongues Becks before returning to Ivegill by means of a network of enclosed tracks and greenways.

Christ Church, Ivegill

The Walk

1 Commence the walk from the car park and with the church to the left side and your back to the village road pass through a gate ahead into a field. Proceed along the right side of the field and once through a second gate continue along the left side of a second field to reach a stile in the further corner. Once over, keep along the left side of a third field to reach a further stile in the far left corner. Turn and climb over the stile into a fourth field then proceed ahead along the right edge to shortly reach a gate. Turn right and pass through the gate and continue ahead gently downhill through a fifth field to reach another gate at the lower boundary. Pass through to reach the Linton Gill access track and turn left.

Between Ivegill and Linton Gill

2 Proceed along the track and where it forks in front of a building take the left track downhill past residential property on the right. Cross over a turning area then, with a dwelling boundary on the right side continue downhill on a grassy path to reach a footbridge and gate at the foot of the slope. Pass through the gate onto a rather boggy woodland path. Shortly turn right, off this path and climb up an embankment by a set of wooden steps and over a stile at the top. Once over, turn right and proceed downhill in a rough pasture to reach a gate at the foot of the slope. Pass through this gate then, with the River Ive now on the left side, cross a wooded area, which includes a low footbridge, to reach a gate.

3 Pass through the gate then cross a paddock area to reach a further gate. From the gate pass over a footbridge, then continue ahead along the left side of a pasture, with the River Ive to the left, to reach a gate at the further side. Pass through the gate then alongside a barn ruin to reach a further gate. Continue then by traversing a riverside pasture to eventually reach a footbridge and stile at the further end. From the stile traverse another short section of pasture then climb over another stile close to a duck pond. From here pass to the left of Beckside Farm to reach a stile close to the River Ive which is set in the fence alongside the final farm building. Veer right, from the stile and cross a field to a gate. Once through, continue close to the river across a pasture which contains short sections of board walk, to reach a stile at the boundary of the High Head Sculpture Park. Climb over the stile into the Park area.

High Head Farm

The Sculpture Park

[Note: At this point in the walk there are two additional opportunities, either or both of which may be followed]

The first is a detailed visit to the **Sculpture Park** (not on Wednesdays). If this opportunity is chosen turn right and follow the path uphill to the Sculpture Park visitor centre and restaurant. Here tickets can be purchased and information obtained about the park before the visit is made.

The second is a visit to the **DEFRA Conservation Walk** of a little over a mile in length. If this opportunity is chosen pass through the small gate ahead and turn left along a track that crosses a bridge over the River Ive. Once over, a sign to the right will indicate *to farm walk and viewpoint*. A 'figure of eight' route can then be followed around fields. This is a 'sculpture trail' using wood carvings from local artist J. Stamper. This trail is planned to be open and available until at least September 2011.

4 **From the stile cross to the small gate ahead.** Once through, cross over a farm access track and pass through another gate into an area containing open air sculptures. Traverse this area by paths, keeping to the right side of a pond. Continue on paths that rise up the right bank, with some zig-zagging, to reach a stile in the far top corner of the sculpture park. Climb over the stile then turn left for a short distance along a track. Cross a small gill then turn off right, up a steep grassy path directed by a yellow sign. Continue on this path, which passes along the top side of woodland to reach a stile on the right just before reaching a dwelling. Climb over the stile and pass by the dwelling (formerly High Head Chapel) across a short left edge of a field to reach a further stile. Once over, turn left and continue along a longer left edge of the field to the far corner, close to an avenue of trees. Turn right at the corner, then continue, parallel with the avenue. Climb over a stile then shortly reach a stile that is set in the left fence. Turn left, climb over the stile, cross an access road through the avenue of trees (this is the access to High Head Castle) then climb over another stile on the further side, into a large field.

[Note: paragraphs 5A & 6A describe a section of DEFRA Conservation Walk which is guaranteed to be available until at least September 2012. If the Conservation Walk becomes unavailable the route described in 5B and 6B should be followed]

High Head Castle was originally a mediæval pele tower of 14th Century origin, which was extended in the 16th Century for the Richmond family. Adjacent to the castle is a stable quadrangle and nearby is a former chapel (now a dwelling), originally of 14th Century origin, which was re-built in the 18th Century. The castle was largely destroyed by fire in 1956, and is now little more than a shell.

Footpath from High Head

5A Proceed ahead across the field and pass to the right of an enclosed stand of trees. Once past the trees veer left and make towards a gate in the left boundary of the field. Pass through this gate and then continue along the right side of a further field. Descend a steep slope within the field and veer left on descent to reach a gate in the lower corner beside the River Ive. Pass through the gate and continue uphill along a right field side, with woodland to the right to reach a further gate. Once through, turn round to the left, then continue on a right handed 'crescent shaped' course across a hillside, with the River Ive on the right side. Pursue this course until eventually a track is joined which leads to a bridge across the river. Cross over the bridge then proceed ahead across a field, with woodland at first on the left side. Once past the woodland veer slightly left to reach a stile in the further left corner of the field.

6A Climb over the stile then continue along the right side of the next field, curving around to the right by overhanging trees. Veer away slightly to reach a second stile at the field edge. Once over, continue ahead along the right edge of a narrow field and over a third stile. Proceed then down the left side of a long field and when the fence veers away to the left continue ahead to reach a fourth stile close to the property Beckfoot. Climb over the stile, drop down a bank onto an access road and cross the bridge ahead over Roe Beck. Turn to the right, along a metalled access road, then curve left around the periphery of a paddock to shortly reach a junction of access roads by the settlement of Thistlewood and turn left.

Thistlewood is a relatively new settlement, with most of the housing having been constructed or renovated since 2000. An important feature within the settlement is the Thistlewood Tower. This was built in the 14th century on land granted by Act of Parliament to the Norman Knight, Thomas de Beaulieu of Thistlethwaite. It later passed into the hands of the Dacre family. The Tower is Grade 1 listed with the adjoining 16th century house. In more recent times the Tower was used to accommodate workers on Thistlewood Farm, before falling into neglect.

5B **Proceed ahead across the field** to reach a gate set in the further boundary fence. Pass through the gate and drop steeply down through rough grassland to reach a stile and footbridge across a small gill. Cross over the gill then veer left up a slope through trees. At the top of the slope climb over a stile into a field, then follow along the left edge to reach a stile in the corner.

6B **Climb over the stile** then continue ahead and downhill through trees. Reach the head of a grassy track and follow this down and round a little to reach a gate and bridge across the River Ive at Thistlewood. Pass over the bridge then turn left, beside dwellings along a metalled access road to shortly reach a road junction and turn right.

7 **From the junction proceed along the access road** to reach a point, immediately beyond the settlement, where there are two adjoining gates. Pass through the right gate onto a gently rising enclosed, unsurfaced track. Continue along this track for about a quarter of a mile to reach a gate at the end of the enclosed track. Pass through the gate and veer right, uphill, across a field towards a point about half way along the further right edge where another field boundary can be seen coming downhill from beyond. Once across the field reach a stile. Climb over this stile, a footbridge and a second stile, then continue uphill along the left edge of a field to reach a gate in the corner, close to the farmstead of Mirkbooths.

Footbridge over Roe Beck

Entrance to The Ashes (above)
... and the way out (top)

8 **From the gate turn left,** along a concrete access road through the farmstead. Pass through a further gate, and continue to a track junction and cattle grid at the entranceway to the residential property 'The Ashes'. Turn left and pass through a gate beside the cattle grid, then veer right and cross over the lawn of 'The Ashes' to a hedgerow gap within the garden. Continue then down the side garden, with a hedge on the right side and pass through a gate. Shortly after, reach a stile that leads from the property into an adjoining field. Climb over the stile then proceed diagonally to the right and downhill across the field. Line up at first with the right end of a line of conifers that can be seen across the valley ahead. Once over the hill brow reach a stile at the field edge. Climb over and continue downhill in the same general direction as before to reach a footbridge in the valley bottom at Roe Beck.

9 **Cross the footbridge** then climb over a stile. Bear right, into rough pasture then locate and follow a path steeply uphill on the left side of a clearing between woodland. Once at the top of the rise continue along the left side of a field with a steep wooded bank to the left. At the end of the field turn sharp left (marked by a yellow direction sign) and descend a steep bank through woodland to reach a stile in the valley bottom of Tongues Beck. Climb over the stile, cross a footbridge over the beck, then rise up steeply on a zig-zag course to reach a field. Continue gently uphill along the left side of the field to reach a gate. Once through, continue along the left side of the next field and pass through a further gate that leads onto an enclosed grassy track. Turn right, along the track and after about a quarter of a mile pass through a gate onto the local road at Intack House and turn left.

10 **Proceed along the road to a junction** and turn left onto a 'no through road' signed to *Sewell House*. Continue along this road for about a quarter of a mile and pass by a *Public Bridleway* sign to reach a metal gate that leads into the farmyard of Sewell House. Cross the farmyard, passing through various gates, then leave by an enclosed concrete access road ahead and rise gently uphill to reach a gate. Pass through the gate, then in a further short distance, when the concrete road turns left, pass through a further gate ahead and continue along an unsurfaced track. At a 'T' junction of paths turn left and pass through a gate onto an enclosed grassy track.

11 **Proceed along this track** and after a short distance turn right and pass through a second gate. A little later turn sharp left with the track, then sharp right, as it passes around and between fields. The track drops gently down to reach a ford and third gate. Once through, continue ahead over a hill brow to reach a fourth gate then drop gently downhill to reach a footbridge across the River Ive at Linton Gill.

12 **Cross over the footbridge** and turn right to reach a gate that was used during an earlier part of the walk. Pass through the gate and proceed up a rough pasture. Pass by a stile that was used earlier and continue along the left field edge to reach a gate close to houses at Ivegill. Pass through this gate then shortly a second gate to reach the village street and turn left. Proceed along the street and after a distance of approximately a third of a mile return to Christ Church and the car park at the end point of the walk.

The origin of **Ivegill** comes from the 'ghyll through which the River Ive flows'. Two main houses in the valley, Ive Bank and The Grange, were homes to Quaker families, with the original small settlement dating back to the 15th Century. The present settlement has spread uphill over the centuries, with Christ Church, designed by London Church architects, RJ Withers & Putney, built in 1868. Further to the east is the Victorian school, which today serves a wide catchment.

Ivegill village

The course of a former railway and hillside paths with commanding North Lakeland views

FACTFILE

Distance
Option A: 4 miles (6.5km)
Option B: 4 miles (6.5km)
Our rating: Moderate

Getting there
Regular hourly public transport from Penrith or Keswick: Routes X4 & X5. Car park and roadside parking in Threlkeld, the walk commencing from Threlkeld Car Park in Blease Road.

Local services
Public houses in Threlkeld village.

Start grid NY318256

Maps
OS Explorer OL4, English Lakes north-western area
OS Explorer OL5, English Lakes north-eastern area

The walk begins in the Blease Road car park in Threlkeld. It passes through the western part of the village before traversing a section of the former Penrith to Keswick Railway along the Greta Gorge. From the railway route it rises up onto the lower slopes of Blencathra, with good viewpoints. The walk returns along an optional lower field path route via the hamlet of Wescoe or a higher route via the Blencathra Field Studies Centre.

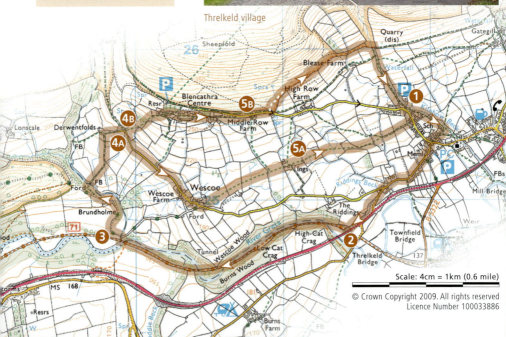

Threlkeld village

Scale: 4cm = 1km (0.6 mile)

The Walk

1 From the car park commence the walk through a gate at the lower, rear corner. This leads onto a Public Footpath signed to *Kiln How*. The path leads downhill beside Kilnhow Beck through a very pleasant wooded dell. Cross the beck, pass through a gate, then cross the beck once again. The path then opens out into a picnic area. Once in this area turn right, up a steep drive and continue to the left side of a dwelling onto a stone based access drive. Continue along this drive, past further dwellings, to reach a junction with Blease Road. Turn left to immediately reach the junction with the main village street near the Public Room. Turn right and proceed along the street for about a third of a mile, veering left at its junction with the side road to Wescoe. As the road reaches its junction with the A66 Trunk Road turn right along the metalled path of the C2C Cycle Route which is signed *Keswick 4 miles*. After a further short distance veer away from the A66 and downhill into Greta Gorge onto the former track bed of the Penrith to Keswick railway. This is signed as *Railway Footpath · Keswick Cycle Path*.

The old railway bridge in the Greta Gorge

2 Once on the former track bed firstly cross a bridge over the River Greta and pass through a gate. Continue along for 1 mile, as the route passes along the gorge. Cross the river a second time, pass through a short former railway tunnel, cross the river a third and a little later, a fourth time. Shortly after the fourth crossing a former lineside hut which is now an information point will be reached. Turn right, opposite this hut, pass through a gate, then proceed ahead to a second gate that leads onto a local access road.

Knott Halloo and Blencathra

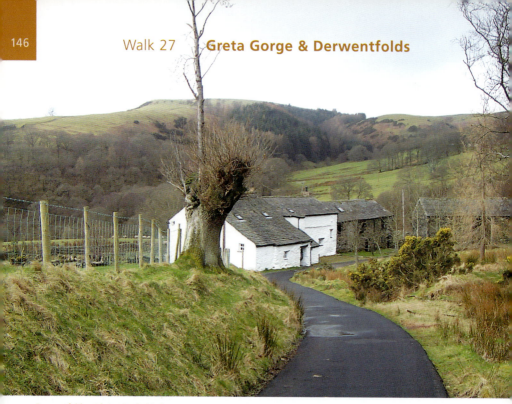

Derwentfolds with Latrigg behind

Footbridge over the Glenderaterra Beck

3 **Turn left, along the road** and rise steeply uphill with Glenderaterra Beck below on the right side. At the top of the rise pass by the property Brundholme to reach a gate. Once through the gate continue a short distance uphill, then veer off the road to the right along a path which is signed *Derwent Folds · Blencathra*. Drop steeply down through woodland, then cross a footbridge over Glenderaterra Beck. Continue uphill, through a gate and along a sunken path to reach a further gate by the property Derwentfolds. Turn right, along the metalled access road to this property and pass through a further gate. Reach a cross junction where the road turns sharply right and footpaths go ahead and to the left.

From this point there are two optional, higher and lower level, routes for the return to Blease Road car park.

Option A – Lower Level Route

4A **Turn right and continue along the access road** as it contours along the hillside for a distance of approximately half a mile, to reach the hamlet of Wescoe. Pass through the hamlet then turn off left, just after a road junction, onto a public footpath signed *Threlkeld 1 mile*. Pass through a gate and proceed ahead across a field to a further gate. Continue in the same direction, across a second field to a stile and a third, which may be a little boggy, to reach another stile. Once over this stile cross a fourth field to reach a gate (and stile) at the property Ings.

5A From the gate pass along a field edge beside Ings to reach a gate at the field corner. From this gate keep ahead and cross a further field to a stile, then another to reach a gate (and stile). Once through this gate veer slightly to the right, pass through a narrow section of field, then keep close to the left boundary to reach a further stile. Once over the stile veer slightly left and cross the next field to reach two optional gates to use. The path then continues along the top left edge of the next field to two further optional gates and the lower right edge of the next to two further such gates close to dwellings in Threlkeld. Pass through and continue along a short length of track to once again reach Blease Road. Turn left and uphill to the car park and the end of the walk.

Option B – Higher Level Route

4B Cross the junction to a gate and stile which lead onto a steeply rising footpath, signed to *Blencathra Centre*. Continue then up the hillside field to reach a gate in the top right corner that leads into rising woodland. From the gate follow a gravel path, through the woodland, to a further gate at the top edge. From this gate veer right, across a field corner, to another gate, then continue along a short section of woodland edge with a fence immediately to the right. Pass through a further gate and shortly after reach the tarmac road within the Blencathra Centre complex.

The path back to Threlkeld

Kilnhow Beck

The Blencathra Centre

Take the left hand upper route between buildings which is signed *Skiddaw House, Blencathra*. At a further junction **do not turn left** at the public footpath sign but continue ahead then veer right (a small white direction arrow should exist) and pass in front of the main conference building of the Blencathra Centre. Once past, continue ahead to reach a boundary gate. From the gate veer left, through trees, then continue a short distance along an old access route to reach a farmstead gate at Middle Row Farm. Pass through the gate and two further gates within the farmstead then shortly after reach the metalled Blencathra Centre to Threlkeld road.

5B Veer right, along the road, for about 200 yards, then veer off left at a *Public Footpath* sign to a stile and gate. Once over the stile turn steeply uphill to the left onto a path signed *Permissive Path* to *Blease Gate Gill*. This path crosses to a stone enclosure wall and then, with the wall to the right side, traverses the hillside below Blencathra. Follow alongside the wall, with good views across Threlkeld towards Clough Head. After about a third of a mile the path drops steeply down and passes through a gate. It then continues reasonably level for a further 250 yards before dropping down to ford Kilnhow Beck. Once across the ford turn right, through a gate, onto an enclosed path with the beck on the right side. A low sign directs to *Threlkeld*. Follow this path downhill amongst trees, drop down steps and cross a bridge over the beck. Continue to reach Blease Road car park and the end of the walk.

Walking
in the
Leith & Lyvennet
Valleys

5

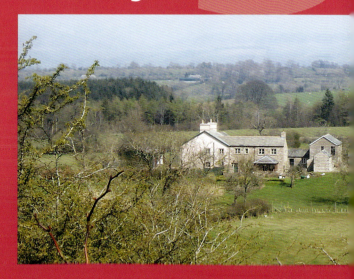

ramblers
at the heart of walking

A walk along forest, field and riverside paths with wide landscape views and a National Nature Reserve

FACTFILE

Distance
7.25 miles (11.5km)
Cumulative height: 500ft
Our rating: Easy

Getting there
Public transport is available hourly from Penrith to and from the entrance to the Whinfell Forest, Center Parcs, Holiday Village (Route 104), from where the walk can commence. Otherwise there is one bus a week, on a Tuesday, from Langwathby to and from Cliburn (Fellrunner Route 562). Parking is available along Cliburn village street with a layby near to St Cuthbert's Church.

Local services
Cafe alongside road from Penrith to Cliburn.

Start grid NY587248

Map
OS Explorer OL5, English Lakes north-eastern area

The walk begins at the main cross roads junction in Cliburn. After leaving the village it traverses field paths and tracks with open views across the Eden Valley towards the North Pennines. It then rises up into Whinfell Forest and follows woodland paths around the periphery of the Center Parcs Holiday Village, to reach the high point of Leacet Hill with panoramic views across the Leith and Eden Valleys to the south and west. The walk descends via the Cliburn Moss National Nature Reserve, to the Leith Valley. It then returns to Cliburn along a Leith riverside path.

The Walk

1 Commence the walk at the road junction that lies at the upper end of Cliburn village street and proceed eastwards, along the pavement of the road signed to *Bolton* and *Appleby*. Once past the houses turn off left onto the metalled access drive to Howgate House, signed as a *Public Footpath*. Veer right with the drive, around the edge of the Howgate House buildings and pass through a gate ahead, onto an enclosed track. Continue along this track, which becomes grassy and pass through two further gates before reaching a third at the end of the track, where it opens onto a field. Continue then along the left edge of the field and pass through another gate at the further side. Follow the left edge of the next field and the following, then pass through a final gate onto a straight unmade access road.

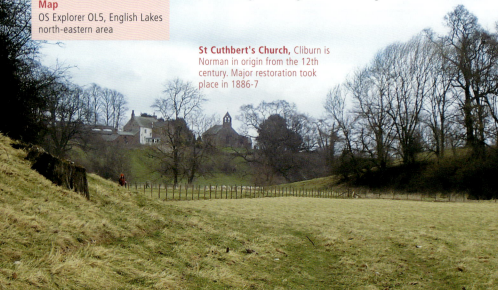

St Cuthbert's Church, Cliburn is Norman in origin from the 12th century. Major restoration took place in 1886-7

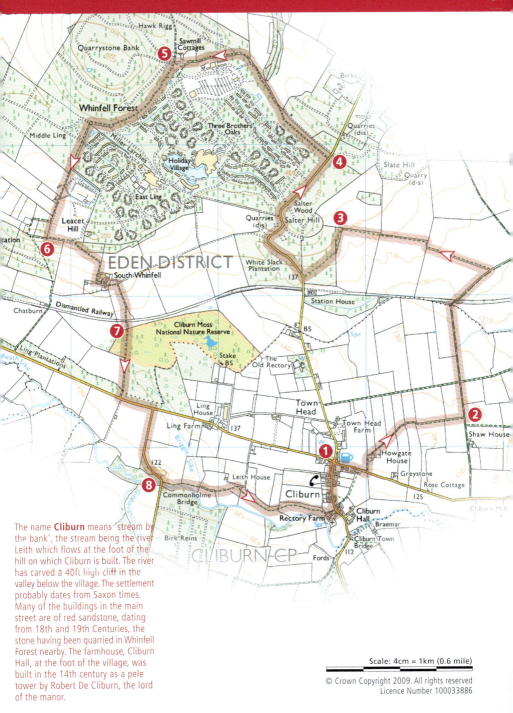

Hawk Rigg

Quarrystone Bank

Sawmill Cottages

5

Whinfell Forest

Middle Ling

Miller Larches

Three Brothers Oaks

Holiday Village

East Ling

Leacet Hill

6

EDEN DISTRICT

South Whinfell

Chatburn

Dismantled Railway

Ling Plantations

7

Cliburn Moss National Nature Reserve

Stake BS

The Old Rectory

Birks

Quarries (dis)

Slate Hill

Quarry (dis)

Salter Wood

Salter Hill

3

4

Quarries (dis)

White Slack Plantation

137

Station House

BS

Spr

Ling House

Ling Farm

137

Town Head

Town Head Farm

Howgate House

Greystone

Rose Cottage

2

Shaw House

125

Cliburn Mill

Leith House

Commonholme Bridge

122

8

1

Cliburn

Rectory Farm

Cliburn Hall

Braemar

Cliburn Town Bridge

Birk Reins

CLIBURN CP

Fords

112

The name **Cliburn** means 'stream by the bank', the stream being the river Leith which flows at the foot of the hill on which Cliburn is built. The river has carved a 40ft high cliff in the valley below the village. The settlement probably dates from Saxon times. Many of the buildings in the main street are of red sandstone, dating from 18th and 19th Centuries, the stone having been quarried in Whinfell Forest nearby. The farmhouse, Cliburn Hall, at the foot of the village, was built in the 14th century as a pele tower by Robert De Cliburn, the lord of the manor.

Scale: 4cm = 1km (0.6 mile)

The **Eden Valley and Stainmore Railway** was built to carry coal and coke across northern England, from east to west and iron ore in the opposite direction. The line was first opened in 1865 and operated for just over 100 years until the Beeching Axe fell in 1962. The engineer appointed to supervise the construction of the Railway and to design its viaducts and bridges was Thomas Bouch, designer of the original Tay Bridge, that collapsed in 1879.

2 Turn left, along the access road and follow it gently downhill, enclosed on either side by walls, fences and hedges. After about half a mile turn sharply to the right, cross the course of the former Eden Valley Railway route (a former underbridge will be seen to the right), pass through a gate, then after a further 300 yards along the track reach a path junction with a route to the left. At this point turn left and pass through a gate, onto a footpath that rises gently along the left side of a field. Continue to the upper left corner of the field and pass through a gateway into the next. Turn right, then left and continue gently uphill along the right edge of the next two fields to reach a stile at the further upper corner that leads into the Salter Hill woodland, which is part of Whinfell Forest.

3 Pass over the stile into the woodland and turn left. Look for then follow a faint path through the trees. To the right the line of a broken wall will be noticed within the woodland. Keep this wall to the right and the boundary fence of the woodland to the left and keep between as they gradually converge. At the point where they join turn right and cross the wall, close to a gate. With the gate then behind you proceed away, along the clear woodland path and after about 300 yards drop down, with the path, to reach a gate at the local road from Cliburn to Temple Sowerby. Turn right, uphill, along the road for about two thirds of a mile. In that distance the road turns sharply on three occasions. It also passes by the emergency exit gates to the Center Parcs Holiday Village and descends gently to a left bend where a woodland footpath turns off to the left signed *Public Footpath Whinfell Forest.*

Sheep near Shaw House

Woodland path on Salter Hill

Center Parcs holiday village was constructed in the 1990's by Lakewoods as a self contained forest village, hidden from general public view. The village accommodates more than 3,000 holiday makers in 700+ chalets within 400 acres of forest. The village boasts about its role as a 'wildlife haven on the edge of the Lake District'. It provides for sports and leisure, including various water based and spa facilities. The village centre includes restaurants, shops, live entertainment, clubs, crèche, bowling and many other activities for its holidaymakers.

4 **Proceed along this path** into the woodland, where the black boundary fence to the Holiday Village will be immediately recognised. The fence is positioned just to the left side of the path and after a turn to the right, with the fence, the path also comes alongside the forest edge. Continue along this route which, though clear, may be a little boggy. After about half a mile along the path from the road turn left with the path away from the forest edge and continue, keeping the black boundary fence to the left side. Keep straight on at a first path junction and later cross over a track junction at a forest clearing where the properties 'Sawmill Cottages' will be visible on the right side. Continue from this junction then turn left to reach the main access road into the Holiday Village. *[Note: This point is the terminus of the 104 hourly bus service to and from Penrith and Carlisle. The walk can be started and finished here. Car parking facilities are not, however, available at this location]*

5 **Cross the access road** to a pair of double gates (green with white top rails) that lead into the forest. Alongside the gates is a small footpath direction sign. Once through (or round) the gates proceed along a forest track with the black boundary fence to the Holiday Village on the left side. This track descends gently with the slopes of Quarrystone Bank on the right side. It gradually turns around to the right and after about a third of a mile from the gates a public footpath sign is reached that directs off the track to the left. At this point a 'private' Lowther Estate notice forbids further public passage along the track. Turn left, as directed by the sign, along a forest path that again skirts the Holiday Village. On this section of path two footbridges are crossed and as it approaches the edge of the forest a very boggy mire is reached beyond which can be seen a stile. Pass through or around the mire then over the stile and continue ahead uphill, with a fence on the left side to reach a stone cross path that leads from the Holiday Village to a golf driving range pavilion.

Leacet Hill. Panoramic views to be gained on a clear day from Leacet Hill include:
• To the west, Blencathra and the eastern flank of the Lake District.
• To the south, the Howgill Fells, Wild Boar Fell and hills around Mallerstang.
• To the east, Cross Fell and the North Pennines.
• Between, the general Eden Valley panorama.

Leacet Hill from Cliburn National Nature Reserve

Cliburn Moss National Nature Reserve is a registered common about 60 acres in extent. The Moss was formed in a hollow left by the last ice age and since then has been affected by man through drainage, peat cutting and planting. It is an unusual example of a low level 'Basin Mire' which is a peat land site that has become extensively colonised with trees. Many of the plant species that occur here are common to fen locations. There is an information board beside the gate that leads into the Reserve.

[Note: If the mire is too difficult to cross turn off the path to the left and shortly reach the stone path that leads towards the driving range. Turn right along this path and re-gain the public footpath at the path crossing near the driving range pavilion]

From the path crossing continue uphill, climb over a stile then continue along a track with a wall on the right side. Pass by a small area of woodland at Leacet Hill in which are located a number of 'pseudo tree' designed radio masts. At the top of the rise reach a 'T' junction of tracks and turn left.

6 Proceed along the track, with panoramic views across the Leith Valley to the south. Continue downhill towards the farmstead of South Whinfell, passing through a gate en route. Where the track passes through a gate close to the farmstead, turn off right, along a grassy path that drops down the right outside edge of the farmstead. Before reaching the last building of the farmstead turn left, pass between barns, then across a concrete apron to reach an exit gate to the farmstead. Once through, turn right at a junction of tracks and continue gently downhill to reach a gate where the track crosses the route of the former Eden Valley Railway. At a short distance beyond this gate the track reaches the boundary of Cliburn Moss National Nature Reserve.

7 Pass through the gate then follow a 'waymarked' path through the Reserve. The path winds through about half of the Moss area and eventually reaches a further gate at the edge of the Reserve. Pass through the gate then turn left, onto the track again and shortly reach a junction with the Penrith to Cliburn road. Cross the road and turn left, along the wide verge area of the road and continue along the verge to a 'T' road junction. Turn right at this junction, onto the road signed to *Newby* and *Great Strickland*. Proceed along this road and drop downhill to reach Commonholme Bridge across the River Leith. Do not cross the bridge but turn left, off the road, onto a riverside footpath signed to *Cliburn.*

8 **Climb over the stile** and proceed along the path with the river on the immediate right side to reach a stile at the field edge. From this stile keep ahead, as the river course moves away to the right and shortly cross over a footbridge. Continue along the left edge of a field to reach a stile in the further corner. From this stile pass around the lower level of a steep bank on the left side, then keep with the path as it climbs diagonally up the bank. At the higher level reach the access track to Leith House, then immediately turn right, away again from the track, and drop down a grassy path back to the pasture land in the flood plain of the river. Continue along the flood plain, immediately below a steep bank on the left, to reach a stile. From the stile continue around the left curve of the next flood plain pasture. At the further side climb up a steep track that leads towards Rectory Farm. At the top of the rise come onto a concrete apron alongside farm buildings. Pass through a gate, turn left and pass through a second gate. Veer to the right then turn right, through a third gate. Pass between farm buildings then turn left, along the main farm entrance road and shortly reach Cliburn village street, close to St Cuthbert's church. Turn left, along the street, to return to the main village cross roads and the end of the walk.

[Note: If you have commenced the walk from the bus terminus at the Whinfell Holiday Village continue by following the descriptions in paragraphs 1 to 4, to return to your starting point]

The **River Leith** rises just to the west of Shap and in its upper reaches flows alongside the West Coast main line to Great Strickland before turning east to Melkinthorpe and Cliburn. It joins the River Lyvennet at Cliburn Mill, which in turn flows into the River Eden at Temple Sowerby. Near Commonholme Bridge a market was held in 1598 at the time when the plague struck in Appleby.

Little used field paths and villages of middle Eden: widescale views and attractive riverside 'parkland' landscape

FACTFILE

Distance
8.75 miles (14km)
Cumulative height: 500ft
Our rating: Moderate

Getting there
Parking is available along the village street in Great Strickland, with a layby beside St Barnabus' Church. There is sporadic public transport to Morland but this is at unsuitable times to serve the walk. The 106 service, every 2 hours (weekdays only) serves the road end for Great Strickland on the A6, about a mile to the west of the village.

Local services
Strickland Arms at Great Strickland; Mill Yard Café and Crown Inn at Morland.

Start grid NY562230

Map
OS Explorer OL5, English Lakes north-eastern area
OS Explorer OL19, Howgill Fells & Upper Eden Valley

The walk begins at the lay-by outside St Barnabus' Church on the eastern edge of Great Strickland village. It firstly traverses the village before leaving along the ancient sunken Maudy Lane. Field paths are then traversed through to Newby Head and on to Morland village. From that village the route passes through woodland and former parkland to reach the Lyvennet valley. It returns to Great Strickland, via Cliburn, by field paths and rough lanes, with widescale landscape views across the Eden Valley.

Great Strickland has historically been staunchly Quaker and was, at one time in the 17th Century, the most important stronghold of Quakerism in Westmorland. The village had no church of its own prior to the late 19th Century, when St Barnabus' Church was built (in 1871) by George Watson of Penrith. The church was built on a low budget, of local materials and is described as being a good example of a sensitively designed Victorian rural church.

Scale: 4cm = 1km (0.6 mile)

Great Strickland. The name is derived from the Scandinavian term for pastureland for young cattle. There was originally one manor of Strickland, divided into Little and Great to distinguish the two parts of the holding.

The Walk

1 With the church to your left commence the walk by passing along the road through the village and once past the Strickland Arms Inn reach the main village road junction and small green. *[Note: This is the point where walkers using the 106 bus along the A6 road, one mile away, will join and leave the walk]* Turn left at the junction onto the road signed to *Little Strickland* and *Shap* and after just a few yards turn off left onto the enclosed path, Maudy Lane. Proceed along this path for about half a mile, at first along the backs of gardens (where it may be boggy), then as a 'sunken lane' between fields. After a while the path winds a little, generally between hedges and en route passes through four gates. Once through the fourth gate turn sharp left and continue along the left side of a field through an informal avenue of trees to reach another gate. Pass through this gate and turn right, then keep around two sides of the next field *[Note: do not climb the stile after the first]* and over a stile in the further corner to reach Inmoor Road.

2 Cross this access road and climb over a stile. Veer right and make across the corner section of a field and over a stone stile on the further side. Continue ahead across the next field towards the premises Field Head. Once over the stile at the boundary of the property keep ahead along the right side of a metal clad building, cross a concrete apron area and pass through a gate to reach a junction of tracks.

3 Pass through a gate and over a stile into the corner of the field which is to the left side of the track ahead. Cross the diagonal of this field and near the further corner climb over another stile into an enclosed green lane. Turn left for a few yards and pass through a gate, then follow along the left side of a relatively low lying field, and through a gate at the further end. Turn left and gently uphill at first, around two sides of the next field (pass through a gateway en route) to reach a gate at the further corner. Once through, continue along the left edge of the next field, and where the wall turns away to the left keep ahead and through a 'funnel' section of field to reach a gate at the further narrow end. Pass through the gate and continue along an enclosed route through the farmstead of Lansmere Farm. Pass through a further gate, veer right and through some more gates, then leave the farmstead over a cattle grid (adjoining gate) and out along a metalled access road.

4 Cross an area of common land, then turn left at a 'T' junction. Pass through a gate, then immediately afterwards a track will veer off to the right side. At this point look ahead across the grassland, bisect the angle between the metalled access road and the track and locate a gate (over 200 yards ahead) in the distance.

Lansmere Farm

Skeels

Newby Head

Make across the grassland and pass through that gate. To the left at this point can be seen the enclosed former Newby Head Quaker burial ground. From the gate locate a cylindrical slurry tank ahead (about 300 yards distant) which is part of Newby Head farmstead. Cross the field and pass to the immediate left of the tank. Once past continue to a gate which leads onto the local road at Newby Head. Proceed ahead, along the road, pass by some barn conversion housing, then at a right hand bend turn off to the left and through a gate, onto a Public Footpath signed to *Morland*.

5 Proceed along the left side of a first field, pass through a gate then continue ahead along the middle of a second and through a further gate. Again continue ahead across the third field, keeping parallel with the field edges and over a stile at the lower edge, near to a lone tree. Turn right, along the right edge of the next field and when nearing a field corner, veer left, along a bank top with a small sike now below to the right. Drop down to the next field corner and ford the sike to reach a stile in the fence on the further side of the sike. Once over the stile, drop down and cross stepping stones over Greengill Sike. Once across, veer uphill to the right and emerge at the top of the slope onto the right edge of a field. Continue along the edge, over a stile and along the edge of the next field to reach another stile.

Morland, approaching Market Square

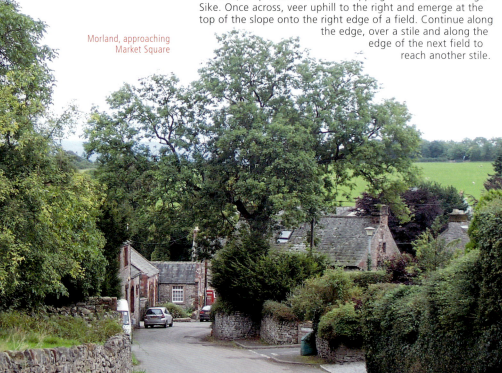

The name **Morland** means 'wood on the moor'. The 11th Century church of St Laurence has the only Anglo-Saxon tower in Cumbria. The main street in the village, Water Street, has a former mill race alongside. The mill wheels driven by the beck over 200 years ago drove mills that produced linen and other cloth. Morland once boasted 3 cloggers, 5 joiner's shops, a bell foundry, 2 mills, a lemonade factory, post office and several grocers' shops. In the Middle Ages Morland was the third largest settlement in Westmorland (behind Kendal and Appleby). When the plague struck Appleby a grant was given for Morland to host Appleby Fair.

6 Once over this stile a wooded dell lies immediately ahead. Skirt around the left side of the dell then once on the other side climb over a stile into a narrow field. Continue then gradually downhill, keeping near the left side of this field. Cross or pass by a footbridge that crosses a side stream then gradually veer to the right to reach a stone wall stile, close to a road, in the lower corner. Once over the stile turn right, along the road into Morland village. At a 'T' junction in the village centre turn right, close to St Laurence's Church. Shortly after turn left and downhill, along the village street signed to *Bolton* and *Appleby*. At the foot of the hill reach the Market Square.

7 Pass through the Square, cross the bridge over Morland Beck and shortly reach a 'T' junction. Turn left here along a local 'no through' road in the direction indicated by a *permissive path* sign. After a few yards turn right, off the road and through a gate, onto a rising grass centred track, again signed as a *permissive path*. Proceed up the left side of a field, then near to the top edge veer left with the track and pass through a gate. Continue along the left edge of the next field to reach a gate at the entrance to woodland. Once through, turn right (not sharp right), off the track onto a rising woodland path. Proceed along this path as it winds between trees and shrubs to pass a high wall corner and reach a gate that leads into a field at the upper edge of the woodland. Pass through the gate, then continue ahead with woodland at first to the left. When the woodland cuts away keep ahead, pass through a gateway then descend gradually along the right side of a field to reach a gate that leads into Hagg Wood.

8 From the gate proceed ahead a short distance along a clear path then turn to the left, with the path, at a 'T' junction with a faint path from the right. Continue then along the length of this narrow woodland but turn to the right, with the path, as it dips and passes into Town Wood. The path (which may be muddy) rises a little to reach a path junction. Bear left at this junction and continue through the woodland, close to its left edge. The path now descends very gradually and after about a quarter of a mile turns left to leave the wood.

Morland Beck meets the Lyvennet near Crossriggs Hall

At this point keep ahead, within the wood, along a lesser path and drop down to a stile that leads out into a valley meadow. Once over the stile cross the meadow ahead to reach the River Lyvennet and a footbridge. Pass over the footbridge, then turn left along a further section of meadow, with the river to the immediate left side. Pass through a gate and keep along a grassy riverside track to come up against the historic iron 'Crossrigg Hall' bridge.

9 **Turn left, cross over the bridge** and continue ahead along a track across former 'parkland'. Pass through a gate then rise up, with a fence on the left side, to reach Winter House at the top of the rise. Pass by this property along a short section of enclosed, gated path then continue, away from the property, along a metalled access road. The road turns sharply to the right about 100 yards past a residential property on the left side. At this point keep ahead, over a stile (or through a gate) and cross a field, vearing slightly to the left to a fence corner that projects into the field. At this point climb over a stile, then continue, in the same direction as before, now along the right edge of a field. At the further corner pass through a gateway then climb over a stone wall stile to reach the Morland to Cliburn road.

10 **Turn right, along the road,** for about a quarter of a mile to reach a left hand bend in the road. At this point continue ahead onto the access road for Akeygate, along a Public Footpath signed to *Cliburn*. Pass to the left side of the property and where the access ends continue ahead, through a gate and along the right side of a field. Pass through a further gate at the field corner and within the next field keep along the right side, turning with the 'dog leg' in the boundary, descending gently downhill. Pass through another gate at the lower field corner, then veer sharply to the left and proceed diagonally down a shallow gulley formation in the embankment landform. On the further side of this field cross a cattle grid (adjoining gate) to reach the local road beside Cliburn Town Bridge. Turn left, along the road, then where it turns left veer off to the right, either across a footbridge or through a ford, onto a signed *Public Footpath*.

Eddy House

11 **Proceed uphill along an unsurfaced track,** at first along the edge of woodland. Pass through a gate (adjoining stile) and at the top of the rise reach a metal field barn. Pass by the barn and through a gate, then continue along the right side of a field to reach a further gate. Once through, turn sharp left and continue along the left side of the next field to a gate in the further corner. From here continue along the left side of the next field to a stile, followed immediately by a ditch that requires to be forded. Continue along the left side of the next field and out through a gate at a 'T' junction of local roads. Proceed ahead along a narrow road for about half a mile to a junction with the Morland to Great Strickland road. Continue ahead, as signed to *Great Strickland* and *Shap* and after a further half a mile reach St Barnabus' Church in Great Strickland and the end of the walk.

Approaching Cliburn

A walk amongst Eden's hidden villages and along a stretch of the picturesque Lyvennet Valley

FACTFILE

Distance
9 miles (15km)
Cumulative height: 800ft
Our rating: Moderate

Getting there
Parking is available in the centre of Morland village and along Water Street on the south side. Public transport is sporadic and at unsuitable times to serve the walk.

Local services
Mill Yard Café and The Crown Inn at Morland.

Start grid NY599224

Map
OS Explorer OL5, English Lakes north-eastern area
OS Explorer OL19, Howgill Fells & Upper Eden Valley

The walk begins in the small square at the road junction in the centre of Morland village. It leaves the village to the south and traverses gently rising field paths to Newby, followed by further paths to Sleagill. It then rises more steeply up to Threaplands, (an isolated farmstead at the junction of no less than 6 rights of way) before turning to reach its fourth village, Reagill. The walk returns to Morland by way of paths that descend to and follow the course of the attractive River Lyvennet as it passes below King's Meaburn and Jackdaws' Scar.

The Walk

1 Commence the walk at the road junction by the small village square in the centre of Morland. Proceed southwards, past the side of The Crown Inn, along Water Street, with the mill race, Morland Beck and the village ford to the left side. After about a third of a mile the road crosses a bridge over the Beck as it leaves the village. Once over the bridge turn off the road to the right and climb over a wall stile onto a public footpath signed to *Newby Road*.

Crossing the ford in Water Street, Morland

Scale: 3.6cm = 1km (0.6 mile)

2 Proceed across three fields, each separated by a stile and keep the Beck on the right side. At the further edge of the third do not climb over the stile but turn right, pass through a gate and cross the Beck by a plank bridge. Once over the bridge turn left and continue round the left side of a large 'L shaped' field. The path starts off within the field heading south and ends along a section of grassy track heading west. Leave this field through a gate (or over a stile) and turn right along the local road and follow it gently uphill to reach a road junction in the centre of Newby village.

3 Continue ahead at the junction, signed to *Little Strickland* and *Shap*, and after about 100 yards turn off left near a post box onto a track which is signed as a *Public Byway*. Pass between properties and after about 100 yards veer to the right at a track junction. Continue along the track, which is enclosed by walls and hedges. Where, after a further quarter of a mile the track appears to be leading ahead through a field gate do not go through but veer to the right of the field and shortly afterwards turn left at a grassy junction of enclosed paths. The path then goes gently downhill to reach a gate. Pass through the gate and continue downhill, but upon approaching Sandwath Beck veer to the right into scrubby woodland to reach an arched stone bridge across the Beck.

Newby means 'New farmstead or village'. This village was once called Newby Stones, a name that probably related to old limestone quarries to the west of the village. The village has a 17th Century Hall, Newby Hall, thought to be on the foundations of an earlier mediæval house. Direction signs in the village are topped with a crown which may recognise the original granting of the manor in Tudor times by King Henry VIII.

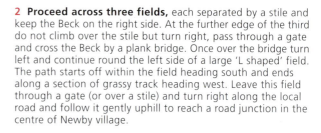

Sleagill means 'Trickling Stream'. The village's recorded history reaches back to C13th. The last Inn in the village closed in the 1940's and shop in the 1970's.

4 **Cross over the bridge** then proceed a little to the right and uphill in a long field. Once the path has risen a little make across to the tree and hedge lined course of Sleagill Beck. Continue gently uphill with the Beck to the left side to reach a stile at the far end. Once over the stile keep the Beck to the left and cross an area of rough grazing ground to a further stile that leads onto a farm track. Turn right, along a track, to reach the Newby to Sleagill road and turn left. Follow along the road for about a third of a mile to reach a 'T' junction in Sleagill village. Turn right at the junction (signed to Shap) and shortly reach seats and a celebratory village plaque and playground.

Bridge over Sandwath Beck

Sleagill. The stone wall stile and signpost to Threaplands (left)

5 **Continue a further short distance** along the road and turn off left, just past a dwelling and climb over a wall stile onto a public footpath signed to *Threaplands*. Proceed along the left edge of a small field and over a stile in the corner near a boggy area. Veer left across the next field to the further side and over a combination of two stiles and a footbridge into the next. Continue ahead in the next field with the boundary at first on the left, followed by an open central section and the boundary later on the right, to reach a gate at the further edge. Keep then ahead, with Threaplands Gill close by to the left, to a stile at the further field edge. Climb over the stile, and then ford the Gill. Once through, continue ahead, with a wall on the right side, to reach a footbridge and stile. From this stile the path rises up quite steeply. Veer slightly right at first, and then take a course that rises left, up the flank of the hillside, with Threaplands Gill down to the right side. Make for a stile which is located in the left 'horizon' boundary fence. Once over, continue in the same general direction as before across the right side of the field and make for a gate in the far upper 'horizon' fence. Once through, continue along the left side of the next field, pass through another gate and make towards Threaplands farmstead and a gate that leads into the farmyard of the property. Pass through this and several gates within the farmstead, the final gate opening into a field in front of the property.

Although an isolated farmstead, **Threaplands** might expect to be inundated with walkers, being at the junction of six rights of way.

Reagill, meaning 'The Ravine haunted by foxes,' was the home of Thomas Bland (1799 to 1865), a home taught painter, musician and sculptor. His garden, known as 'The Image Garden' in the centre of the village, is Listed and has a range of his sculptures, now somewhat weathered. During the reign of Queen Victoria an annual festival was held in the garden to celebrate her accession to the throne.

6 Turn left and cross in front of the property to reach a wall stile on the further side of the field and access track. Once over the stile proceed along the left side of the field to reach a metal gate at the far side, a little way to the right of the field corner. Pass through the gate and descend at first along a rough track in a narrow field. As soon as the track begins to rise, veer off it to the right and cross the field on the diagonal to reach a wooden stile set in the right boundary. Climb over the stile then proceed diagonally at an angle of about 30° away from the boundary. Cross rough pasture and pass by some hillocks that have resulted from earlier mining activities. After rising a little continue downhill towards Reagill. Proceed towards the village street and eventually reach a metal gate alongside a small red post box. Pass through the gate onto the village street and turn right.

7 Proceed along the village street for a few yards then turn left at a 'T' junction, signed for *Appleby*. Continue gently downhill between two walls to reach a second 'T' road junction. Cross over this junction and pass through a gate onto a signed Public Footpath. Proceed along the right side of a narrow field and climb over a stile at the further end. Continue along the left side of the adjoining narrow field to reach a stile and gate, then along the left sides of the next two, separated by a stile. Pass through a gate then continue ahead, veering slightly to the left to reach a stile and footbridge where the footpath reaches the woodland area of Hard Bank. Once in the woodland the general direction of the path veers to the left, towards the further left corner about a quarter of a mile distant. In practice there is a series of yellow direction signs that mark out a zig-zag route through the woodland. This course should be followed but if this proves difficult always move towards the left. The path emerges from the woodland along a length of track, to reach the Maulds Meaburn to Morland road. Turn left, along the road to reach a junction, on a corner, with the metalled access road to Lowfield Farm.

Lowfield Farm

8 **Turn right** and proceed along the access road. At a corner, after about 100 yards, turn off left, through the left hand of two adjoining gates. Continue along the right edge of a field to reach a combined footbridge across a ditch and stile. Once over the stile proceed ahead and downhill but veer slightly to the left across an area of springs and water issues. The path then shares a narrow route between field fences, with the water course. Where the fences open out a deep channel needs to be crossed ahead. This can be achieved by first skirting a spring or issue to the right then moving ahead to reach a rough access track. Turn left, along the track, and continue to the entrance gate to the property 'Turnbank'.

[Note: A footpath diversion is in prospect here. If it has been put into place turn off right before the gate, through a gate (or over a stile) and continue to a gate in the field corner. Once through continue between farm buildings and through a further gate, then veer left across a meadow and over a gill. Turn right to reach a footbridge and stile, close to the River Lyvennet at the far end of the meadow. Continue then from **]

9 **Pass through the gate** and cross a footbridge to reach a track junction. Turn right, then left between barns, to reach a gate that leads out of the property. From the gate proceed along a riverside meadow to reach a footbridge and stile at the further right corner, beside the River Lyvennet.

**Keep then close to the river and next cross a rough planted area to reach a second stile. Continue below trees then rise up a little to cross two stiles in quick succession, followed by a further area of rough pasture amongst trees. At the edge of this area climb over a stile onto a roughly metalled road and turn right to reach some stepping stones by a ford, across the River Lyvennet.

The **River Lyvennet** flows for a little over 12 miles from its source at Black Dub on Crosby Ravensworth Fell to meet the River Eden near Temple Sowerby. The countryside around the full length of the river is picturesque. In its upper reaches the river flows through villages such as Crosby Ravensworth and Maulds Meaburn whereas, by virtue of its incision into the landscape in its middle stretches, it passes below villages such as Kings Meaburn.

River Lyvennet near Turnbank

10 Cross the river using the stepping stones then continue uphill along the road. Pass through the farmstead of High Whitber to reach a stile and gate on the left that lead onto a public footpath signed to *Walltree Brow* and *King's Meaburn*. Turn sharp left onto the footpath and drop downhill to a footbridge. Cross over the bridge then veer left, across the slope of a hillside field and through a gate at the field edge. Continue ahead, below a wooded embankment to reach a stile close to the River Lyvennet. Once over the stile keep alongside the river, climbing over stiles, where necessary, to avoid land slips. Pass by the end of a footbridge across the river, then towards the end of a narrow meadow rise up to a stile in woodland. Once over the stile continue downhill again and over a further stile to reach the access track to King's Meaburn Mill. Cross over the track and continue on a meadow path alongside the river. Pass through a gate into riverside woodland and then out again over a stile to reach the King's Meaburn to Newby road beside a ford.

The bridge and ford at King's Meaburn

11 Cross over the road and pass through a gate onto a riverside track signed as a *Public Footpath* to *Morland*. Proceed along this track, with the river to the left, past a dwelling and below an impressive rock cliff known as Jackdaws' Scar. After curving round with the river pass through a gate (or over a stile) then continue on a riverside path around the left perimeter of a pasture area. At the end of the pasture climb over a stile into an area of riverside woodland. Pass through the woodland, which slopes steeply up to the right but take care over numerous tree roots. At the edge of the woodland climb over two stiles in fairly quick succession to emerge in a further long area of pasture which is flanked by the river and hillside woodland. Proceed ahead along the length of the pasture then, as the woodland closes in again, pass through a gate (or over a stile) and continue along a section of track to reach a path junction beside Chapel Bridge.

On the west side of **Chapel Bridge** there used to be a place called Chapel Garth, with a chapel dedicated to the Blessed Virgin. This disappeared many years ago, although 'Chapel Well' still exists on the site.

The name **Morland** means 'wood on the moor'. The 11th Century church of St Laurence has the only Anglo-Saxon tower in Cumbria. The main street in the village, Water Street, has a former mill race alongside. The mill wheels driven by the beck over 200 years ago drove mills that produced linen and other cloth. Morland once boasted 3 cloggers, 5 joiner's shops, a bell foundry, 2 mills, a lemonade factory, post office and several grocers' shops. In the Middle Ages Morland was the third largest settlement in Westmorland (behind Kendal and Appleby). When the plague struck Appleby a grant was given for Morland to host Appleby Fair.

12 Turn left, pass through a gate and cross over Chapel Bridge. Continue uphill and then pass to the left side of the property Kemplee *[Note: a footpath diversion is in prospect at this location]* to reach a 'T' track junction. Turn right, then shortly left at another junction and pass through a gate onto the main access track to the property. Proceed along this enclosed track, which gradually rises uphill. The track turns a number of times, passes through a gate and by the property Highgate Farm. After a distance of a quarter of a mile the track reaches the Bolton to Morland Road. Turn left, along the road, then at a road junction keep ahead and downhill to pass between dwellings and reach the ford and footbridge at Water Street in Morland. Once over the footbridge turn right, along Water Street, to reach the centre of the village and the end of the walk.

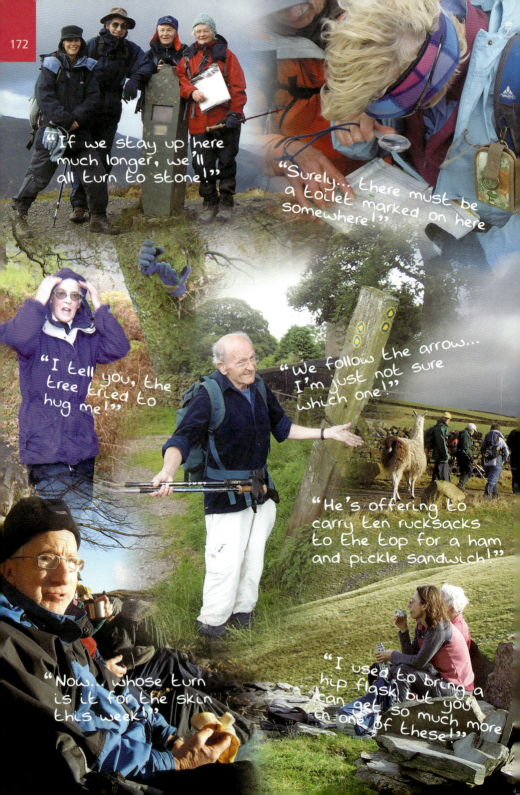

172

Walks in the
Penrith
area

A selection of 30 walks
to celebrate the 25th Anniversary
of the Penrith Group of Ramblers

Ullswater & the Eamont valley
The Lowther valley
The Eden valley
Countryside north & west of Penrith
Leith & Lyvennet valleys

Written and photographed
by Graham Allan

Designed and produced
by Mike Cooper

with assistance from
members of Penrith Ramblers

Spring 2010

Walks in the Penrith area

First published 2010
Updates and expands upon
Walks in the Penrith Area:
Book 1 *(March 1989)* and **Book 2** *(May 1990)*

Published by Penrith Ramblers Group
© Penrith Ramblers 2010

Researched and written by Graham Allan
with additional walk surveys by
members of the Penrith Ramblers group

Designed and produced by Mike Cooper
Photographs and maps by the authors

The mapping in this book is reproduced
by permission of Ordnance Survey on
behalf of HMSO
© Crown copyright 2010.
All rights reserved.
Licence number 100033886

ISBN: 978-1-906494-15-5

Printed in Penrith by Reeds Printers